W. Herbert Thomas

Mormon Saints

W. Herbert Thomas

Mormon Saints

ISBN/EAN: 9783743334311

Manufactured in Europe, USA, Canada, Australia, Japa

Cover: Foto ©Thomas Meinert / pixelio.de

Manufactured and distributed by brebook publishing software
(www.brebook.com)

W. Herbert Thomas

Mormon Saints

MORMON SAINTS

BY

W. HERBERT THOMAS

LATE OF THE

"*San Francisco Examiner*"

AUTHOR OF "THE AMERICAN INDUSTRIAL SYSTEM," "NIAGARA,"
"AMERICAN MINING CAMPS," "THE CHINESE IN 'FRISCO,"
ETC., ETC.

WITH ILLUSTRATIONS

London:

HOULSTON AND SONS,
PATERNOSTER SQUARE
MDCCCXC.

PREFACE.

THE History of the Mormons contains many strikingly interesting features; and speculation as to the probable future of the Church in the United States is being freely indulged in by those who have watched the actions of the unbelievers in regard to the Latter Day Saints. The Supreme Court has recently decided that the dissolution of the Church under the Edmund's law was constitutional ; so that as a corporate body it has ceased to exist, and its property is to be administered by Federal officials. Those who continue to practise plural marriage are being rigorously imprisoned, and the latest ' revelation ' has caused the abandonment of the teaching of polygamy. The Gentiles are out-numbering and out-voting the Mormon dwellers in Salt Lake City. Will the repressive legislation and the influx of Gentiles, weaken the hold of the faith upon the minds of the present followers of Joseph Smith and Brigham Young; and prevent the accession of youthful converts to the Church ? What are the characteristics of the Mormons ? Are they misguided fanatics or vicious people ? How should they be treated by those whose views are antagonistic ? Is polygamy still secretly practised ? Is the faith a rational one, or based on superstition ? What lessons may be drawn from this history of bloodshed and persecution, and the struggle to found a settlement in a strange land? I have approached these questions as an enquirer ; and this little work is a study, not an exposure. I have aimed at accurately reporting what I saw and heard whilst among the Mormons, and at compiling other facts so that the discussion of the questions raised might be thorough and impartial. How far I have succeeded I leave the careful and unprejudiced reader to judge. There are said to be fully twenty-five thousand Mormons in England alone, while in America there are claimed to be several hundred thousands, so that it can scarcely be unprofitable to examine the faith to which they are proselytes, and the customs which are in vogue among them. I have set down nothing in malice, but have endeavoured to show both the light and shade in the picture. I hope the Latter Day Saints, as well as the Gentiles, will give as dispassionate consideration to the evidence I have collated as I have bestowed labour in endeavouring to bring up Truth from the bottom of her Well.

W. HERBERT THOMAS.

Penzance,
    Cornwall,
        October, 1890.

CONTENTS.

MORMON SAINTS!!

CHAPTER I.

"And Solomon had seven hundred wives and three hundred concubines, and his wives turned away his heart."—I Kings xi. 3.

BURNING QUESTIONS.

SOCIAL AND RELIGIOUS PROBLEMS ARE THE STUDY OF THE AGE.

WHILE the few are speculating as to whether or not life is worth living, the many are seeking to discover how our existence may be brought to harmonise with the divine intentions. In the upheaval caused by the investigation of social evils, moral systems and religious faiths have to stand at the bar of criticism, and show cause for their existence. Human happiness is dependent upon our living under rational and natural social conditions; and upon our being in touch with the Master Mind of the Universe.

We want to know what we must *believe* as to the life beyond the visible; we desire to know what we must *do* as moral beings, capable of thought and action.

B

Consequently the claims of the various religious creeds are the subjects of keen controversy and careful analysis ; while ethics engage the attention of an equally vast number of students, who deal with established rules of conduct in a manner which implies that re-adjustments of codes are necessary when man's development changes the conditions of his life.

Some may regard the discussion of the question ' Is marriage a failure ? ' as a trivial and meaningless specimen of journalistic sensationalism. To me it implies that the relations of the sexes in the marriage state are seriously discordant in a great number . of instances. The causes of this conflict are being ascertained with more or less exactness ; and although love and marriage are as old almost as the Garden of Eden, the ventilation of these complex questions should be continued until the complete solution is attained.

LOOK BEFORE LEAPING.

Before any important innovation is allowed we should entertain no reasonable doubt as to the wisdom of the proposed change ; for it may be that in many respects our ideal is true, and our attainments only failures because of individual carelessness or wilfulness.

A certain class of theorists advocate free love, which means an utter abolition of our existing marriage laws ; while the mildest of that school plead for a return to the polygamous system, which was in vogue among the ancient Hebrews, as a panacea for the evils which they attribute to unnecessary restraint in the conjugal state. As polygamy, or plural marriage, has been one of the most striking features of the religion of the Latter Day

Saints, an examination of the practical working of that system may enable lovers of truth to draw a better comparison between our own monogamous institution and that which we are asked to sanction, if not to adopt.

The religious aspect of the Mormon community is equally novel and curiously interesting. We have professed Latter Day revelations to Joseph Smith, the founder of the sect, and to Brigham Young, his successor; accompanied with alleged supernatural manifestations, which have successfully appealed to the faith or credulity of hundreds of thousands of converts. It is useless to pooh, pooh, the question, of whether the religion is of divine origin, for as faith is demanded by all religious creeds, almost any belief that affects the hopes and fears of the people will have its advocates. It would have been unwise if christian theologians had refrained from answering the arguments of the rationalist critics, for men are persistently demanding either demonstrations or logical polemics ; and it would be equally dangerous to ignore the claims of any church to the faith of the masses, who soothe their minds by clinging perhaps to the most transparent delusion, until a purer and more rational religion is set before them.

The Mormon saints interested me so greatly that, while in Salt Lake City a year ago, I interviewed several of the prominent Mormons and Gentiles ; and since then have made an extensive investigation of works on the subject. In the following pages I shall give the result of my own labours ; together with condensations of the statements of other writers, so that from a perusal of the whole, the public may find satisfactory answers to the questions which will suggest themselves to all who feel an earnest desire to have an accurate knowledge of the lives and beliefs of their fellow men.

WHERE THE SAINTS LIVE.

It was early morning when we steamed into the depôt. The commodious and detached houses, amidst well-kept gardens and waving trees (which also lined each side of the avenues); the wide streets along which sparkling water flowed from the hills around; the towering edifices and apparent fertility of the soil, all indicated that this home among the mountains, if not an abode of the blessed, was at least a blessed abode.

The sun was gleaming on the purple hills; fruit blossom and beautiful bright-hued flowers perfumed the air; silvery waters gleamed in the distance; on some of the hills the snow still rested, although it was almost summer, and the sky was cloudless.

No fairer city could one wish to behold; and yet in 1847 when the Mormon band came down Emigration Canon they saw only a wilderness in which they must live if they wished to escape assassination. So they pitched their tents, and in less than fifty years by dint of hard labour and perseverance they made the desert give birth to the rose. Irrigation and energy did the work, for the climate is usually so dry that without assistance from man the soil would not have been productive.

Standing boldly against the clear atmosphere were the most striking edifices of the city—the Mormon Tabernacle, and the new Temple of the Saints. The spires of the Temple, the flat roofs of the houses, the air of tranquility that pervaded the city, the scarcity of women in the streets, and other features, impart, as

Max Adeler remarks, "a truly oriental aspect to the scene." The bustle of an American city is absent, and because Salt Lake city is different from any other settlement in the United States, it is as interesting to an American as to a European.

CRIMINALS AND TRAMPS.

" Some people imagine," said our guide, " that compulsion is used here to recruit the Mormon Church, but this is false. They recognise the right of everyone to freedom of thought, speech and belief. There are ten or eleven religious denominations in the city, and there is not the slightest interference from anyone."

As we passed the gaol, he remarked that in this prison the new steel rotary cells were in vogue, so that the prisoners' actions could be watched all the time, and any scheme to escape be frustrated. " Of the criminals " he continued, "fully 85 per cent. throughout Utah territory are from the ranks of foreigners, the remaining 15 per cent. being drawn from the Mormon population. The population of Utah is 230,000 ; and of Salt Lake city 32,000, of whom 27,000 are Mormons, the proportion holding good throughout the territory, so that the Saints, even with their bad reputation, hold the law in greater respect than the other inhabitants."

WORK FOR THE LAZY.

"We have no paupers here," said he, "for the country around is prosperous, and we have a sure cure for tramps. If any shiftless mortal comes along who prefers idleness and penury to honest labour and the regular wage, we quickly spot him and give him three or six days at the gravel bank in return for his board and lodging, with the result that the aristocratic tramp usually passes by Utah with a cold and haughty air; or being once amongst us is glad to shake the dust of the modern Zion from his feet."

Pointing to a very fine building, the guide said as we stopped our vehicle for a moment, "this is St. Mary's Academy, a Catholic school for girls. There is also a similar institution for boys. There are ten or twelve outside schools which have no connection with the district schools. In the latter no reference to Bible or Deity is made, and there is a school in each of the twenty-one districts into which the city is divided. The territory also owns an Academy."

Passing a Mormon mansion, the residence of Mr. Hill, the cashier of the Zion Savings Bank, the guide said that the stock of the bank was worth 300 per cent., and perhaps, could not be bought for that.

I was impressed with the fact that whatever might be the condition of the working classes, the heads of the Mormon Church seemed to be rolling in riches. Their houses and grounds were as magnificent as those of any wealthy men in other parts of the world. That of John Taylor, the late president of the Mormon Church, and successor of Brigham Young, was a pretty fair specimen. The guide said that Taylor was in Carthage gaol when Joseph Smith and his brother were assassinated by a mob, while under the protection of the State of Illinois. Taylor, Smith and others were then in confinement on account of their having advocated polygamy; Taylor having four wives.

POLYGAMY NOW A CRIME.

The result of the strong popular feeling against Mormonism has resulted in polygamy being prohibited by law, so that it is now a crime to live with more than one wife.

"On this side," said the guide, pointing to another dwelling "resides George Q. Canon, who has five times represented the Mormons in Congress. Only recently he emerged from the penitentiary where he served a term for refusing to desert his wives, whom he had married before the passage of the Edmond's Bill, which compelled men to put away all except the first wife. He was the only member ever unseated because of his advocacy of Mormon customs. Since the passage of the bill 900 convictions have been secured in Utah Territory. The penalty is six months in the penitentiary, and a fine of three hundred dollars. The law is carried into effect most rigidly, and the practice of polygamy is almost extinct."

Our next halting place was a spot which is the greatest attraction to visitors to Salt Lake City, viz., Temple Block, on which are situated the Mormon Temple and the Tabernacle. The former is not yet completed, although the gigantic task was commenced on April 6th, 1853, and no less than $2,000,000 (£400,000) were expended in erecting the walls of granite, which was obtained from the Washatch range of mountains at the back of the city. In addition to this up to the present time it has cost a similar sum in the construction of the remainder of the building, so that the total cost will be enormous. It is 200 feet by 100 feet; the walls are 100 feet high, and the middle tower on each end will be 200 feet. It is built entirely of granite.

THE EAGLE GATE.

HEARD A PIN DROP.

By the side of this massive edifice is the Tabernacle, which was designed by Brigham Young, and its erection superintended by himself, about twenty-two years ago, at a cost of $300,000. It looks something like an immense oval beehive, its construction being very peculiar. It will seat 12,000 persons, and can be emptied in two minutes by means of the twenty doors that open on the court-yard, so that admirable precaution has been taken against loss of life by fire. It is built of wood, is 250 by 150 feet and 70 feet high, being one of the largest buildings in America without a central support. The wood used in the roof is ingeniously crossed and dovetailed, and the acoustic properties of the Tabernacle are remarkable. One of the officials whispered from the rostrum at one end and he could hear him distinctly from the gallery at the further end, a distance of 200 feet ; and we also heard a pin drop into a silk hat which he held in his hand. The gallery extended all around the building, and was supported by a single row of pillars. Instead of lamps being placed in different parts, the Tabernacle is lit by a row of gas jets around the bottom of the front of the gallery. The seats were of light-coloured wood, and so arranged that the whole congregation faced the preacher. It is said that the appearance of the inside of the vast dome was not pleasant to the eye, and this has been remedied by draping the interior with long streamers of evergreen and coloured paper. In the centre was suspended a huge floral piece ornamented with small American flags, presumably emblematic of the loyalty of the Mormons to the Stars and Stripes. Services are held every Sunday at 2 p.m., when a sacrament of pure water is administered; after which the Saints adjourn to the Theatre or elsewhere; as the drama, dancing and other amusements are not prohibited by their religion.

The organ in the Tabernacle is one of the finest in the world, being forty feet high, and containing 2,648 pipes. It cost $100,000. This place of worship has a mixed choir of 120 voices.

CHAPTER II.

" But they which shall be accounted worthy to obtain that world, and the resurrection from the dead, neither marry nor are given in marriage."—Luke xx. 35.

BRIGHAM'S PARADISE.

THERE seems to have been some doubt as to how many wives Brigham Young actually had. Artemus Ward states that some persons said "there was about eighty of her," while others placed the number at twenty. I asked one of the elders in the Tabernacle, who said he did not know the total number, but that Brigham Young, shortly before his death, had stated in his presence that he (Brigham Young) had sixteen wives living, and forty-three children.

"This building," said the guide, stopping before a large plain edifice, "was once a tithing office ; now it is a general storehouse. The tithes in Utah are voluntary contributions, no compulsion whatever being exercised towards those who may feel indisposed to yield up a tenth part of their earnings to the church, after the old Jewish fashion ; but the delinquents are few. The tithes may be paid, either in land produce or money, to the head Bishop. By means of this system, and the establishment of Relief Corps for charitable purposes, no one throughout the territory is compelled to beg, and, in fact, we have no beggars amongst us."

Not many minutes after we had dispensed with the guide, I may observe in parenthesis, a fairly decently dressed lad asked us for money, as he said he was destitute; but then " it is the exception that proves the rule."

SEIZING THEIR PROPERTY.

The Amelia Palace, named after Brigham's alleged favourite wife, was another evidence of the lavishness of the wealthy Mormons. It cost '$100,000; is provided with all modern conveniences, in the shape of elevators, heat radiators, etc., and is elegantly furnished. It was erected for the use of the Presidency of the Church, but is now in the hands of a Receiver, together with several large farms, thirty thousand head of sheep, and other property, seized and taken from the Mormons for violation of a section of the Edmonds Bill, prohibiting the retention of more than $50,000 worth of property, besides places of worship, by any religious society. An appeal has been taken to test the constitutionality of the act.

The Zion Co-operative Mercantile Institution which we glimpsed in passing was twenty rods long. It was started by Brigham Young in 1869, and has a business of from four to six million dollars annually, and a capital of $1,250,000. The stock is worth $115 on the market, $40,000 worth having changed hands at that figure two weeks before I was there (April 12th, 1889). Two hundred persons are employed in the establishment, some of whom make boots, overalls and jumpers. Later on we paid a visit to the Store, which had a glass roof, admitting light to all the galleries, and gained a better idea of its magnitude.

WHERE THE PROPHET DIED.

We next passed through the Eagle Gate; four pillars uniting in the centre to form an arch on which was perched the " patriotic piece of poultry " which is the brazen emblem of America's greatness. This was the gateway to Brigham's block of school-houses. We were shown a window of the Lion House, the Prophet's chief residence, from which he used to gaze around the city after dinner, and wonder on which of his wives he should next bestow his caresses. In a room to the north he died on August 29th, 1877, being 76 years old.

The residences of his first wife and one of his sons John W. Young, were handsome stone buildings, surrounded by gardens in which grew tulips and hyacinths. This son is the third male offspring, and he is a very enterprising railroad man, owning two or three branch railroads leading out of Salt Lake City.

There are also a number of houses in which sons, grandsons and other relatives of the deceased Prophet live ; as they were handsomely provided for at his death. He is said to have left a comfortable home and a sufficient fortune to support each wife during her lifetime, and $20,000 to each of his forty-four children. Ann Eliza, his last wife, however, left Salt Lake and went throughout the country preaching against Mormonism. She was only between twenty and thirty years old, so this was truly one of the May and December marriages, few of which are productive of happiness or contentment in our own country.

SEE TWENTY MILES.

From the Eagle Gate a splendid view can be had of

GRAVE OF BRIGHAM YOUNG, SALT LAKE CITY, UTAH.

the City, and the range of mountains beyond; as the road goes as straight as an arrow to its foot, a distance of twenty miles, and the air is so light that objects scores of miles away can be seen plainly with the naked eye.

Brigham sleeps inside the rails which enclose a grave-plot on the side of a hill. His monogram is engraved upon the gate.

A plain stone lies over his remains, which occupy the south-east corner of the plot. He desired no monument; being more modest on quitting the world than when alive; but, as the guide said, "This entire city, with its 100 miles of streets 120 feet wide, its Temple, Organ, Co-operative Stores, etc., is a standing monument to his name."

Later in the day in conversation with another citizen, the latter said he was present when Brigham Young was interred. Under the coffin, which was of native wood, was a sandstone slab, and the huge block of stone above it weighed several tons.

Four of his wives lie in separate graves alongside of their common husband, and as some of the survivors are now old and wrinkled it is probable that after a while he will be surrounded by more of his earthly treasures.

SHE STOOD ON HIS GRAVE.

An adventurous young lady from Boston (The Hub of the Universe) immortalised herself when the rest of our party left the spot, by climbing over the high rails, in order to plant her dainty foot on Brigham Young's tomb.

" This house with the three chimneys," said the voluble guide, "is the residence of John T. Kane, the present representative in Congress. The chimneys are a sign that he is not a Mormon.

" The mines at the back of the mountains around the city are very rich, eight million dollars having been paid in dividends by the Ontario mine. The value of Utah's mineral product for 1886 was ten million dollars. Fort Douglas, where the soldiers are garrisoned, is three miles east of the City.

" When the Mormons were driven out of Illinois in 1847, after suffering horrible privations, fourteen men and three women came down Emigration Canon opposite, and formed a settlement, which was rapidly augmented by saints from other parts of the world.

" Irrigation being necessary for fruit growing and other purposes, seven streams now flow down the hill-sides into the Jordan river to the west, and the soil is now most productive. The streams are formed by thé melting snow."

THE WHEAT AND TARES.

Outside the house of the third wife of Bishop John Sharp several Mormon children were playing on the grassy bank as happy as any English children. Sharp only lives with the first of his wives as the law annulled his other marriages, and declared the children illegitimate. In the next building to this residence lives a man who settled on the same spot in early days in a tent, which has now given place to an elegant villa.

" You will observe," said the guide, as he pointed to Mormon and Gentile houses in proximity—" That the great antagonism between the Saint and the Sinner exists only in the imaginations of newspaper correspondents, for they live within a few yards of each other. I came here in 1848 myself, and ought to know something of the facts of the case."

I would have liked to take a trip to the Great Salt Lake, but it is about sixteen miles from the city; and I should have been obliged to neglect a more important object which I had in view.

WANTED A HUSBAND.

An American whom I once interviewed in San Francisco said, " I have just come from Salt Lake City, and I like some of the scenery in that region. Garfield Beach on Great Salt Lake is a most beautiful spot, and as for the Lake itself the water is so salt and heavy that a well-built man could lie on his back and go to sleep on the water without sinking."

He added a sweeping and uncompromising opinion of Mormons. " I have no use for Mormons," said he, " The men are short and insignificant, while the women are ugly and illbred. One woman told me that she would marry a man if he were married to another woman and had no love for herself."

The following graphic description of the Lake, and the pleasure of bathing in it, is taken from the "Detroit Free Press ":—

BATHING IN THE LAKE.

" Bathing in the Great Salt Lake is an experience so unique, so delightful and exhilarating, that it can never be forgotten. There is probably nothing like it in the world. It differs entirely from ordinary salt water

c

bathing. The water of the lake is so extremely heavy (being nearly 29 per cent. salt) that a person cannot sink. It is really a strange sensation to one who is not accustomed to bathing in this water to walk out into the lake. You feel yourself growing lighter and lighter as you advance, until you seem to weigh nothing, and it is only with the greatest difficulty that you can keep on your feet. The feet, being lighter (ordinarily) than one's head, show such a decided determination to come to the surface that one is rather startled, and you immediately picture to yourself the dire calamity of your feet in the air and your head under the water. But no such state of affairs ever exists. After you have become accustomed to the buoyancy of the water, you will probably do as the others do—that is, you will let your feet come to the surface, when you will find yourself calmly floating on the water with your head and shoulders entirely above. The body is gently rocked as the waves roll in and softly break upon the sand. By lying on the back and placing the arms at right angles to the body and drawing them down to the sides, the bather can propel himself rapidly through the water with comparatively little exertion. The bathing season commences in June, and lasts until the latter part of August, the temperature of the water varying at different months during the summer, ranging from 60° to 85°, reaching the latter point during August.

CLOSE YOUR MOUTH.

" The area of the lake is 2,000 square miles, it being seventy-five miles long by fifty miles wide in the widest place. The average depth is probably about fifteen feet, the greatest depth being about thirty-five. There are two bathing resorts, Garfield and Lake Park. Trains leave the city for the lake at nearly all hours of the day. The favourite, or rather the fashionable, hours of the day in which to bathe are from 3 to 5 o'clock p.m., between which time the water is the warmest. Notices are posted in every corner cautioning bathers not to get the salt water into the mouth, nose, or eyes, as it is very disagreeable and irritating ; and if allowed to get in the lungs is extremely painful. But with ordinary caution there is little or no danger. It is a common sight to see two hundred people lying quietly on the surface of the water without the least exertion.

ROWING AND SUNSETS.

" The beach is composed of a remarkably clean white sand, and the water is as clear as crystal, the bottom being clearly discernible at almost any depth. The lake is well supplied with rowing boats for the accommodation of the public. There are also two strong rowing clubs on the lake—the Garfield Club at Garfield, and the Salt Lake Club at Lake Park—and the contests between the rival clubs have never failed to attract large crowds. Owing to the extreme buoyancy of the water, boats float one-third lighter than in fresh water, and therefore it is claimed that the water in Great Salt Lake is the fastest in the civilized world.

" The view from the beach is beautiful at any time, but reaches the climax at sunset ; when the islands and the distant mountains assume the varying tints of the sunset sky, and the surface of the lake looks like a vast basin of molten silver, quivering in the slightest breeze. The tints are so delicate, and the view so inspiring, that once seen it makes a lasting impression upon the memory."

THROUGH PREJUDICED SPECTACLES.

Here is another description of the great Salt Lake :—
" From Salt Lake City to Ogden the railway traverses
a narrow plain. On the one side are the dead waters ;
on the other the sharp peakes of the Washatch Range.
The region is highly cultivated. Farms reach their
brown or green fields over its length and breadth, and
little streams run in bright threads out of the mountain
Cañons and across the meadows. And the lake itself !
Always mysterious, it appeals to the imagination of
every traveller. It sleeps for ever. No waves dance
over it, no surf roar breaks the stillness about it. Is it
sulky, one wonders ? Does it recall the time when its
waters covered the whole of Utah ? Is it jealous of the
mountains about it, remembering when they were battled
against ? What history belongs to it ? Why has it
alone remained part of a mighty ocean, salt and lifeless ?
The high peaks are radiant and full of life ; but the lake
is dull and heavy.

CHAPTER III.

"True love in this differs from gold or clay,
That to divide is not to take away."
                THE FUTURE OF MARRIAGE.

UNFAIRLY TREATED BY STRANGERS.

The main idea I had in view was to secure an introduction to one of Brigham Young's score or so of
widows, or at any rate to interview her if I had to
introduce myself. I first hastened to the office of the
·"Salt Lake Herald," the leading Gentile paper, and laid
my difficulty before the Editor, who received me very
kindly.

"I am afraid that you are attempting an impossibility,"
said he, "seeing that your train leaves in a few hours.
However, I will assist you as far as I am able. Several
of Brigham's widows are in town at present, I believe;
and I am personally acquainted with all of them, but I
dare not introduce a newspaper man into their homes."

"Why?" I asked.

"Because they are adverse to having their private life
made the subject of curious enquiry of strangers," he
replied. "They have a certain religious belief, and they
are as modest and conscientious as any people under
the sun. Several persons have from time to time
abused their confidence in this manner, and they would

be sure to feel aggrieved if I were to bring them into unpleasant notoriety."

" But is there no one to whom you can introduce me, who will in turn secure an interview for me with one of the widows ? " I suggested.

YOUNG BRIGHAM.

After some reflection and consultation with his sub-editor, my new-made friend rang up some of the Prophet's sons on the telephone, who were, however, not in their offices at that moment. They were expected back shortly, so in the meantime I placed the Editor on the witness stand.

" I am like a good many other people," said I, " more interested in, than informed about, Mormonism. Do not the Mormons claim that their religion is of divine origin through revelations to Joseph Smith, the founder of their sect ? "

" They certainly claim, and believe it firmly too—" he replied—" Joseph Smith and Brigham Young were both from Vermont, and the former started Mormonism in New York in consequence of the alleged finding of some gold plates by him (through revelations), on which were inscribed certain characters, which being translated proved to be the Book of Mormon."

" Well, seeing that the polygamous system is the main point in which Mormonism appears to differ from other religions, I would like to know whether or not it operates, or has operated successfully ? "

FORTY YEARS OF POLYGAMY.

" They have had forty years of this kind of thing," was the reply, " and as far as I can judge they have got along all right on account of their genuine belief, in the majority of instances, that they were obeying the will of God. If the conscience is obeyed, even though the actions may be opposed to natural inclinations, persons usually obtain as much happiness as fall to the lot of man. There is practically no new polygamy, now that it is made a criminal offence, so we have to do with plural marriage as a thing of the past. To me Mormons are pretty much the same as other people. They carry out, or try to carry out, their own peculiar ideas, and as everything with them is voluntary they seem to have no more discord than marks the lives of other religious enthusiasts."

" Did the wives live together ? "

" Only in rare cases ; as it is understood that a man must not take a wife until he can support her, and as a rule the men with most wives were middle-aged men who could keep up separate establishments, and they did so. Sometimes the increase of families rendered this imperative, but often one wife has reared the children of another, if the first died, or the other had no children."

" How do the children themselves seem to view the matter ? "

" As most of the inhabitants here are Mormons the home training has that tendency, so it is not surprising that the majority grow up in the same faith, and consider it perfectly natural to do as their parents, provided it were lawful. The same result is usually found in any community where the religion is not a mere matter of form, or for use only on state occasions."

" I noticed the Zion Mercantile Institution." I remarked, " Is that the property of the Mormon fraternity,
or merely a co-operative body similar to those in
England."

"Originally it was purely co-operative, as those
Mormons who started it worked and divided the
profits, but now it is more of a stock company, and the
employees are paid the market value of their labour,
and no more. There is nothing socialistic whatever in
the arrangement.

MORMONDOM A COMMUNE.

" In theory Mormondom is something in the nature
of a commune, but in practice human nature is the same
as in other parts of the world. The saints call each
other ' brother ' and ' sister,' but if a man can make
more money than another he keeps it. Hence we have
rich and poor as in other communities, and in some
instances in the past when a poor man has burdened
himself with three or more wives with whom he has lived
in a rough log cabin, the poverty has been very keen. But
this is an exceptional case, as precautions are usually
taken to prevent, or alleviate, absolute destitution.

" For instance, a year or two ago the County built a
house two or three miles below the city, and bought a
farm, on which they have taken care of several poor
families. They have a system here among the Mormons
of each Church Ward taking care of its own poor out
of the district tithes and contributions."

" Is Salt Lake City prosperous ? "

" Yes, the outlook is very favourable, although we
have occasional stagnation of trade. There is very

little unemployed labour in the city. We depend for our prosperity upon mining, agriculture, and manufacturing, there being numerous machine shops in full swing."

" What is the average rate of wages ? "

" At present miners earn [in English money] from 12/- to 18/- per day; mechanics, carpenters, etc., 12/- ; day labourers, 6/- to 12/-"

" It seems to me," I suggested, "that a great deal of energy is devoted by the Mormons to increasing the population, in direct opposition to the Malthusian theory that there are too many people in the world at present for the amount of wealth produced ; or, at any rate, that population constantly tends to increase faster than wealth ? "

MORE CHILDREN, MORE GLORY!

" You have struck the right idea," replied the Editor, smiling, " for the object of life with Mormons is to procreate. The more children you have, the greater your glory will be hereafter ; so that they partake more of the character of the old Hebrew women, who thought it a disgrace to be barren, rather than of the Parisian or even American type, who often think children objectionable, to put it very mildly."

Further conversation was stopped by the use of the telephone again, but without avail, and the Editor closed the interview by saying : " There is one chance for you yet to see one of the widows. I will send you up to ' Aunt Em,' who runs the " Woman's Exponent." She is one of the wives of Daniel H. Wells, one of Brigham Young's councillors. She is one of the cleverest Mormon ladies, and can, if she will, give you the introduction you desire."

Armed with Mrs. Wells' address I set out again on my mission. I was convinced by the fact that the Editor was extremely cautious in his replies, that the dark side of Mormonism, if there was one, must, perhaps, be sought from someone outside the locality where the Saints are in the ascendency.

A TYPICAL SMART MORMON LADY.

I glanced at Mrs. Emmeline B. Wells rather critically, for she was supposed to be an educated Mormon lady, and would undoubtedly show more striking traces of the effects of the system upon a refined nature, than an illiterate and superstitious person, ready to grasp at any bait which tempted her credulity.

Mrs. Wells was apparently between fifty-three and fifty-eight years of age, small, wiry, grey-haired, and neatly dressed. But what struck me most were the lines across her forehead and cheeks ; furrows that scarcely looked like the wrinkles produced by age ; but rather by a life of stern struggle with something which had embittered her cup of happiness ; drinking dregs that were utterly distasteful, yet never shrinking, because considering it a matter of duty, as pilgrims have done penance by walking with blistered feet to some ancient shrine, suffering, yet smiling through their agony. The firm chin and tightly-drawn mouth hinted of a strong will, ready either to conquer self, or to attack those opposed to her. Something in her voice too sounded hard and metallic at times, and yet on the whole she was pleasant and hearty, and I liked her. I believe her object in life was to *be* good and to *do* good. From her writings, which I afterwards saw, I found she was very fond of poetry, and that the name ' Aunt Em' over which she wrote was not a misnomer. She found her own happiness in making others happy.

" What is the character of this paper you edit ? " I asked, after introducing myself.

" ' The Woman's Exponent,' " she replied, handing me a copy, " is a journal published in the interests of the Rights of the Women of Zion, and the Rights of the Women of all nations. We claim the right of Female Suffrage, which has been taken from us because we are Mormons, and voted in accordance with our conscience."

" Do you claim that Mormonism tends to elevate the condition of woman ? " I asked.

" Certainly," was the reply. " I am aware that many persons who do not know us think that we are slaves ; but nowhere in the world has woman more liberty than under our religion. She is respected, is accustomed to think for herself, lives as noble a life as any woman, and usually has a higher sphere of labour. We have our Women's Societies and Clubs for our improvement and pleasure, and everything is done to give women an object in life, rather than fritter away her valuable time in the frivolities of fashion and gaiety, although we do not condemn any innocent amusement and recreation.

HOW THEY CRUSH JEALOUSY.

" But is not plural marriage, as you term polygamy, demoralising in its tendency ? Is it not repugnant to woman's natural instincts ? "

" I will answer your last question in the affirmative. It is natural for a woman to desire to absorb all of a man's affection, for human nature is intensely selfish. How far this desire would have operated but for the monogamous training through which we have passed for centuries, cannot be estimated; but now, as the result of our environment, woman is accustomed to think her husband must live to consult her wishes in all things, and devote his time and love exclusively to herself. But we introduce the element of Spiritual Duty into our lives ; and while seeking female emancipation where we are bound by legal fetters, we obey a higher code of morals, and for conscience' sake crush our natural infirmities and evil passions. We believe that our prophets were inspired by God, and we consider it our duty to obey the commands delivered unto us."

" Suppose," said I, " that in a vision, or by any other medium through which the Mormons receive their revelations, you were ordered, or believed you were, to sacrifice human life, would you kill a child to offer up a sacrifice, as Abraham was prepared to do with Isaac ?"

" That is rather an extreme case," said Mrs. Wells, smilingly ; " but I believe we should do as we were told, if we were convinced that the command was of divine origin. We have stood the weight of obloquy that has been heaped on us by other nations, and we should not withhold our own lives if they were needed by the Lord. But I don't think such a test is necessary, or would ever be imposed on us in these days."

Mrs. Wells propounded my question to several other Mormon ladies of good standing who were in the room ; but they said the matter had never been raised before, and they could not, therefore, pass an opinion as to what course would be taken.

" How do you Mormon wives get along together ? " I enquired.

" More happily than blood relations do with you," she replied. "This young lady," pointing to an amiable, fair-haired, and fair-complexioned girl, who acted as her sub-editor, " is one of my husband's daughters by another wife, and we have never had an angry word in our lives. Mr. Wells has, or rather *had*, six wives ; for now by law he has none, his first wife being dead. We all love each other, and consider each other as belonging to one family. We have much to bear, however, for if my husband were to enter my house this minute he would be arrested. In fact fathers have been sent to prison for merely following a dead child to the grave. We are under the strictest surveillance, as though we were great criminals ; but we consider it a part of our duty to be loyal American citizens, and we do not violate the law. We believe that force is no remedy. We must convince the world that celestial marriage is pure and productive of good, and show by our lives that we are not as black as we are painted."

MUST KISS THEM ALL.

" How about the husbands, though ; do they never display favouritism to the younger and prettier wives?"

" If they are true to their faith they do not. They ought not. A man cannot—or rather could not, for we must remember that plural marriage is illegal—marry a new wife unless his previous wives consent, under the laws of the Church, so he should be as kind to the elderly ones as to the younger ones, and he usually is. My husband is one of the best of men. Sometimes, of course, a man does display partiality, for there are bound to be some undutiful persons in any society."

" If a man takes his wife for a drive does all of her go at a time ? " I enquired.

"No, he usually takes one only, and the others wait until some other time. In the same way.he visits them according to arrangement with them. If he kisses one he is supposed to kiss all on going away on a journey."

Mrs. Wells then gave me her autograph and several pamphlets about the church. After some persuasion she informed me where I should find Mrs. Zina D. H. Young, one of the most intelligent of Brigham's widows, but she did not feel justified in introducing a stranger to her. " These widows are very much like other people " said she, " I don't see why you are so anxious to talk to one. There are the pictures of two of them on the wall."

I replied that because of Brigham Young's position his wives were certainly curiosities. The photographs were those of two ordinary looking women, neither very young. And, by the way, I do not remember seeing a single really good-looking girl in my perambulations about the streets of the city : possibly they were kept indoors.

Mrs. Wells's house is flanked on one side by the old fort, an *adobe* house, built by Brigham Young in 1847; and on the other side by a stone house, which was used as a mint to coin the gold that was brought there from California in 1848, during the beginning of the great gold fever.

At that time the Indians used to live there in their wigwams. There are still some of these children of nature "with untutored minds" around the city, but their flat, bloated, copper-coloured faces ; black, matted hair ; and their gaudily coloured blanketed forms, make them far from sightly objects.

CHAPTER IV.

___

"There is beauty all round when there's love at home."

___

MRS. YOUNG INTERVIEWED.

When in the tabernacle I purchased one of Brigham Young's portraits, an engraving of which forms the frontispiece. He does not look much like a prophetic dreamer. He is not angelic enough. It is a portrait of a very large, stout man with a massive head. His large brow indicated him to have been what he really was—a clever, shrewd man—while the strong nose and firmly-set mouth and chin, as surely showed that he was born to command. His eyes were small but keen. A short white beard ornamented the lower part of his chin, and his hair, of silver grey colour, was inclined to curl. Altogether I should say from his picture that he was a man whose animal passions moulded the bent of his ambition. The life of an ascetic would have had no charms for him, for nature had moulded him differently.

Contrary to my expectation I met with a polite reception from Mrs. Young, to whom I apologised for intruding upon her privacy.

" Come inside," she said, cordially.

The house differed in no respect from those of well-to-do persons in our own land. The drawing-room, into which I was ushered, was furnished with taste, the walls being hung with oil paintings, some of which were portraits. Money had neither been lavishly expended, nor penuriously withheld, in fitting up the apartment. Comfort and refinement had been combined.

·OLD BUT VIGOROUS.

The description of Mrs. Wells would almost apply to Mrs. Young, except that the latter was several years older. The same wrinkles and air of firm repression; the same shrewd look and staid affability; the same willingness to talk when treated with deference, and the same evident desire to proselytise; 'duty' the one actuating principle governing conduct; were noticeable to the close observer.

I determined that my interrogatories should be mainly directed to her reasons for upholding polygamy, as I had only casually dealt with this part of the Mormon religion in my previous interviews.

" I desire to know more about your religion, Mrs. Young," said I; "but will you first tell me something about your late husband? Did you live with him long?"

" Thirty years is long enough to study a man's character," was the reply, " and I lived with Mr. Young that length of time. A more loving father, or a kinder husband never lived on earth. He was honoured and loved by myself and his other wives, as well as by the whole Church. I had three children by him, and raised four belonging to another wife when she died. One of the latter's children is inside now, and another, you may notice, is just passing the house. Mr. Young's character has been vilified throughout the world. They have even accused him of murdering people, but it has been our lot to be persecuted and maligned because we seek to elevate the race by living pure lives and propagating the true religion. We have suffered, but our cause is increasing in strength, and no power of man will ever exterminate us or our Church."

" What is the basis of your religious belief ? " I asked.

" We believe," said she, " in the Old and New Testaments, together with the later revelations made to Joseph Smith, the Prophet, known as the Book of Mormon."

" How was it that Joseph Smith founded the Church of the Latter Day Saints ? "

JOSEPH AND THE ANGEL.

" I see," said Mrs. Young, " that you are not familiar with the writings of our people. But I can give you a brief history of the origin of the Church. Joseph Smith, whom I knew well, and knew him to be a godly man, was born in New York, and educated to the Presbyterian faith, as I was myself. But early in life he became conscious that he was to do a great work. He wandered about the mountains for four years nourishing that spiritual life within him by agonising prayer, living among the Indians, and purifying his mind and heart of worldly dross. It was then that the Lord revealed unto him the place where he found the gold plates, in a stone box, on which were engraved strange characters.

" Joseph could not decipher these characters, so he took them to a professor of languages, who said the writing was in the old Hebrew style. It was translated, and the result was the book of Mormon. The plates were seen by Oliver Cowdery, David Whitmore and Martin Harris, who were also convinced of their divine origin; because an angel of God came down from heaven and laid the plates before their eyes; and they have so testified in a preface to the book. Eight other witnesses saw the writing and the translations, and they swore before God that they lied not.

THE PROPHET MURDERED.

" Joseph was commanded to establish the Church of Christ on earth again, and to raise up a race of God-fearing people. The result was martyrdom for him and his brother; for after being involved in thirty-nine law suits they were decoyed by women and killed. My husband was with them but he escaped. Because of our belief we have been hunted from one place to another by the government of the United States, but we fear neither man nor devil as long as we do what is right. We were driven out of Courtland, Missouri, at the point of the bayonet, but the time will come when we shall be exalted above all men."

" What is the religious belief of the Mormons in brief, Mrs. Young ? "

For answer the lady handed me a card on which were printed the Articles of Faith of the Church, which read as follows :—

WHAT THE MORMONS BELIEVE.

1.—We believe in God, the Eternal Father, and in His Son, Jesus Christ, and in the Holy Ghost.

2.—We believe that men will be punished for their own sins, and not for Adam's transgression.

3.—We believe that through the atonement of Christ, all mankind may be saved, by obedience to the laws and ordinances of the Gospel.

4.—We believe that these ordinances are: First, Faith in the Lord Jesus Christ; second, Repentance; third, Baptism by immersion for the remission of sins; fourth, Laying on of hands for the Gift of the Holy Ghost.

5.—We believe that a man must be called of God, by "prophecy, and by the laying on of hands," by those who are in authority to preach the Gospel and administer in the ordinances thereof.

6.—We believe in the same organization that existed in the primitive church, viz.: apostles, prophets, pastors, teachers, evangelists, etc.

7.—We believe in the gift of tongues, prophecy, revelation, visions, healing, interpretation of tongues, etc.

8.—We believe the Bible to be the word of God, as far as it is translated correctly; we also believe the Book of Mormon to be the word of God.

9.—We believe all that God has revealed, all that He does now reveal, and we believe that He will yet reveal many great and important things pertaining to the Kingdom of God.

10.—We believe in the literal gathering of Israel and in the restoration of the Ten Tribes. That Zion will be built upon this continent. That Christ will reign personally upon the earth, and that the earth will be renewed and receive its paradisic glory.

11.—We claim the privilege of worshipping Almighty God according to the dictates of our conscience, and allow all men the same privilege, let them worship how, where, or what they may.

12.—We believe in being subject to kings, presidents, rulers and magistrates, in obeying, honoring and sustaining the law.

13.—We believe in being honest, true, chaste, benevolent, virtuous, and in doing good to ALL MEN; indeed, we may say that we follow the admonition of Paul, "We believe all things, we hope all things, we have endured many things, and hope to be able to endure all things. If there is anything virtuous, lovely, or of good report, or praise-worthy, we seek after these things."—JOSEPH SMITH.

"Everything we believe, uphold, or practice," said Mrs. Young, "is found in the Old and New Testaments."

" Then you claim that polygamy is sanctioned by the Bible ? " I enquired.

SOLOMON'S MODEST FAMILY.

" I claim that you will not find one word between the covers of the book condemning it. We believe that the Bible says what it means and means what it says. Polygamy was practised by David, who was considered the man after God's own heart ; by Solomon, the wisest man of his time ; by Abraham, who also had intercourse with Divinity, and by other great biblical characters. I know the old cut and dried argument ' that God permitted this and many other things because of the hardness of men's hearts ; but other vices, crimes or sins were denounced and penalties laid down by God.

" Christ knew when He was upon earth that polygamy was practised in Judea at the time when he preached against adultery, hypocrisy, drunkenness, and other sins, yet He never uttered a word on the subject. Many passages of scripture contain the word ' wife ' and not ' wives,' but merely because the plural is not used it does not follow that no man can marry more than one wife. Besides this the prophet Joseph Smith teaches us that it is right in the sight of God."

MORE CHILDREN, MORE GLORY.

" What other arguments have you in favour of polygamy ? " I enquired.

" We desire to raise righteous children to counteract the evil in men at the present time, and we believe that the more children there are born in a spiritual and eternal union the greater will be our glory hereafter.

The wives can help each other in the rearing of the children and comfort each other in trouble. There were fourteen wives of Mr. Young alive at one time, and we lived together until the growth of families made it necessary to form different households. Several other wives were sealed to him although he never lived with them. I do not know the total number of his wives, but we found that plural marriage begat a nobler love towards our husband and to each other.

MONOGAMY A BLIND.

" On physical, moral, and social grounds we uphold polygamy. Society, as at present organised, is a whited sepulchre. Wherever monogamy is the prevalent marriage system it is but a cover for sin. Men are false to their vows, and ruin themselves, besides degrading their families, by supporting a class of fallen and depraved creatures who would not exist if all women could get married to good men without having contumely heaped upon them. If men do not violate their vows they are cruel to their wives, because unwillingly, or physically unable, to practice the necessary restraint during certain periods, when it is absolutely necessary for the preservation of the health of the mother. It is for this reason that one husband is sufficient for a woman, while a man requires several wives.

MARRIAGES OF CONVENIENCE.

" The very people who denounce us, wink at the infamous product of their own system. If all men did their duty in the world there would be no great necessity for plural marriage; but as it is there are more women than men in most civilised countries, and what marriages are contracted are usually not pure, or a part of religious life, but merely legal unions for selfish purposes."

"It seems to me," said I, "that your system is very convenient for the men and very self-sacrificing for the women. Would not the same men who now gratify their passions by faithlessness to their one wife, use the plural system for the same unholy purpose if they adopted your religion? Is it not selfish on the part of men to desire more than one wife?"

NO HAPPY HUNTING GROUND.

"If you imagine that the care of a large household of wives and children is merely amusement for a man you are mistaken," replied the lady. "If a man undertakes the responsibility and joins our church from a base motive, his actions will soon speak for themselves, and he will be known to the church as a hypocrite. We are temperate and virtuous as a whole; although evil-disposed persons have at times joined our society. For ten years there was not a drunken man, nor a house of ill-repute seen in this city. We detest immorality as much as any sect, and unless a man is united to a woman by a spiritual bond he is expelled from the church. If he abuses his wife and thereby shows that his profession is but a cloak, she can obtain a divorce, for women's rights and liberties are better preserved in Mormondom than elsewhere. Plural marriage is not compulsory with us. Some individuals will only desire, and be only able to support, one wife, but there are thousands of women who must lead lonely lives unless they can contract an honourable marriage with a God-fearing man.

MORE MONEY, MORE WIVES!

"The question of wealth enters largely into the matter, I should imagine," I remarked, "for the wealthy men can have all the wives they want, while the poor men must be content with one, no matter how much love they may have for the female sex. You do not then believe in an equal distribution of wealth?"

"We each mind our own business," replied the widow, "taking care, of course, to prevent destitution in any family. There is no community where all men are equally endowed. All men have different degrees of ability, varieties of temperament and tastes, and we put no artificial obstacle in the way of industrial progress by imposing restrictions on the ownership of wealth. As a people we have been abundantly blessed, in spite of the persecution of our enemies."

"What is your attitude towards other Churches?"

"We believe that all men will be saved who do not deny Christ or sin against the Holy Ghost."

Before I left the house Mrs. Young pointed out the portrait of Joseph Smith, which, if faithful, showed the prophet to be a fine-looking man with clean shaven features, a rather long thin nose, benevolent expression, and with long hair thrown back from a high forehead and tied behind in the old Puritan fashion. He was a contrast to Brigham in every way.

Mrs. Young furnished me with her autograph, saying that the "H." in Zina D. H. Young stood for Huntingdon; all the prophet's wives ending their maiden names with "Young."

The Mormons, I noticed, preserve the names and addresses of their visitors, for here, as well as at the

office of the " Woman's Exponent," I was requested to
conform to the custom.

BRIGHAM'S DAUGHTER'S VIEWS.

A few extracts from a recent article in the " North
American Review " by Mrs. Susa Young Gates, one of
the children of Brigham Young, will fittingly follow the
statements of Mrs. Zina Young. She says that Brigham
was the father of fifty-six children, all of whom were born
healthy and without " spot or blemish " in body or
mind. Thirty-one of the number were girls ; twenty-
five were boys. Seven died in infancy, three in child-
hood, seven more since reaching maturity.

Mrs. Gates contends that polygamy produces as
beneficial results among human beings, as it does in the
breeding of quadrupeds. She says :—

" As a physiological fact, of the fifty-six children born
to Brigham Young, not one was halt, lame or blind, all
being perfect in body and sound of mind and intellect ;
no defects of mind or body save those general ones shared
by humanity. The boys are a sound, healthy, industrious,
and intelligent group of men, noted everywhere for their
integrity and for the excellent care and attention bestowed
upon their families.

" The girls are finely developed physically, quick and
bright in intellect, high-spirited, and often talented,
especially in a musical way. All are nice girls, kind in
disposition, generous and social in their natures."

Plutarch, in his " Life of Lycurgus," anticipates that
similar effects would follow variety of sexual relations in
the case of women as well as of men. He remarks :—

RATIONAL REGULATION RECOMMENDED.

" When he (Lycurgus) had established a proper regard to modesty and decorum with respect to marriage, he was equally studious to drive from that state the vain and womanish passion of jealousy, by making it quite as reputable to have children in common with persons of merit, as to avoid all offensive freedom in their own behaviour to their wives. . . . . . Lycurgus considered children not so much the property of their parents as of the state; and, therefore, he would not have them begot by ordinary persons, but by the best men in it. In the next place, he observed the vanity and absurdity of other nations, where people study to have their horses and dogs of the finest breed they can procure either by interest or money; and yet keep their wives shut up, that they may have children by none but themselves, though they may happen to be doting, decrepit, or infirm. As if children, when sprung from a bad stock, and consequently good for nothing, were no detriment to those to whom they belong, and have the trouble of bringing them up; nor any advantage when well descended and of a generous disposition."

The Mormons, however, vigorously insist that their women shall remain faithful to one man.

Referring to Brigham's polygamous household, his daughter gives an idyllic picture of the family life, especially waxing eloquent over the evening prayer, when "ten or twelve mothers with their brood of children would gather around the family altar;" forming a goodly congregation in themselves. She states that these Mormon wives were pioneers in a new order of things, " whose tears watered into existence the lovely

flowers of unselfishness and charity." Instancing one
patriarch, she says :—

A PERFECT HOME.

" Nothing could exceed the sweet gentleness with
which this father of twenty babies watched and guarded
every separate " bit " of humanity that came near him.
I have been with this man, too, when he first enjoyed
the companionship of a young, beautiful bride. Not a
whit more devoted or tender was he to her than he had
been and was to the cherished wife of several years ; he
was to each and every one all that a true, affectionate
husband could be.

" Nowhere on the face of this wide earth is the love
of husbands for their wives, and wives for their husbands
so intense, so thrilling, and so divine as it is here in Utah.

" Statistics will bear me out in saying that there are
fewer paupers, fewer criminals, fewer insane among
polygamous than among monogamous families. It is a
well-known fact here in Utah that there are fewer
physical defects and greater intelligence in plural homes
than in the same grade or class in monogamy."

These Mormon women she claims " are working
grandly at the sex problem of the nineteenth century,"
their maternal relations make it possible for a mother to
move out on independent lines in business, in art, and
the professions. The wife spends the twenty years of
the child-bearing period in rearing her children and in
quietly studying and preparing for a wider mission when
she can add the weight of her experience to the great
problem of humanity. Mrs. Gates adds, " That polygamy, wisely and faithfully practised, will be a grand

factor in the bringing to pass this millennium of usefulness and happiness, I sincerely believe."

Mr. W. T. Stead, commenting on this article in the "Review of Reviews" says, "As there are nearly three-quarters of a million more women than men in the United Kingdom, there is *prima facie* more force in the argument for modified polygamy than for any other experiment that has been put forward by the advocates for inter-meddling with the relations of the sexes." Hence he considered there would be more tolerance for Mrs. Gates' plea for polygamy than for Mrs. Mona Caird's advocacy of free divorce.

CHAPTER V.

" I saw plurality at its best, and I give it to you at its best. I have shown the silver lining of this great social cloud. At the back of this silver lining the cloud must be thick and black, I feel quite sure."

ARTEMUS WARD.

THUS far nothing I have written has shown the Mormons in an unfavourable light. The editor of the Gentile newspaper said nothing against the saints, and, as might have been expected, Mrs. Wells and Mrs. Brigham Young warmly defended the church from any imputations made by their opponents. In order to form a just idea of the Mormons and their religion, the other side should be studied equally as carefully, and the evidence weighed with an unprejudiced mind.

I had to leave Mrs. Young rather abruptly in order not to miss my train, but I was fortunate enough to fall into conversation immediately afterwards with Superintendent White, of the Spring Valley Grammar Schools, San Francisco, who was on his way to Europe to see the Paris Exhibition, and to study the social and industrial problems of the different European Countries. He had spent a longer time in Utah than myself, and his observations showed that he had used his time and discerning power to good advantage.

" Morality," said he, " is merely a question of longitude and latitude. It is as natural for different nations to have different systems of morality as varieties of language and facial peculiarities. So I only try to study the effects of these differentiations, without condemning the people wholesale because my own ideas of right and wrong differ from theirs.

THREE STORIED HEADS.

"I attended service at the tabernacle last Sunday afternoon," he continued, "and watched the Mormons flock into the court-yard. They were a fairly representative gathering. There were the few men and women of intelligence·and position in the church, and the great mass of poor, low-browed, superstitious-looking followers, with long upper lips and dull eyes. There were no 'three storied heads,' like Sir Walter Scott's, in the place. Many of the men had miserable-looking horses and carts, rope being used instead of leather traces in some cases, and the attire of these believers was shabby in the extreme. There was a stolid, heavy expression of countenance such as you always find among persons ready to become proselytes to any religion which is placed before them in a plausible or fanatical manner.

IGNORANCE AND SUPERSTITION.

"On enquiry I found that the majority of these men and women were of the more ignorant classes of English, Irish, and Scandinavians, with a few Scotch ; no Italians, Spanish, or others of the Latin race being among them, and very few Americans ; Joseph Smith, Brigham Young, and a man named Morgan having been almost the only prominent American members of the sect. None of them looked very bright or happy.

"As a rule in religious gatherings a large preponderance of women is noticeable; as they are naturally more reverent or superstitious than men. But I was struck with the large number of men in this Mormon congregation, showing that they are as much dominated by feeling or faith as their wives. Apostle George Q. Cannon, their ex-Member of Congress was the speaker, and throughout three-quarters of the address I could close my eyes and imagine myself in some old Baptist Church, the teaching was identical; but towards the close a tirade against the government for persecuting the sect was indulged in, and the women were instructed as to their duty to their husbands. It was Cannon's first sermon since being pardoned by President Cleveland while serving a term in the penitentiary for polygamy.

MORMON PATRIARCHS.

" I noticed too the extreme longevity of the Mormons. President Woodruff, the head of their Council, is eighty-two years old, and speaks with the vigor, intellectual grasp and heartiness of a young man. Most of the apostles are grey-haired men, and so are many of the rank and file, which is pretty conclusive evidence that they are a temperate and active people. The girls were not remarkable for beauty, and from what I could gather a great many of them would prefer marrying Gentiles to Mormons."

DEFECTIVE EDUCATION OF CHILDREN.

" As an educationalist I visited their schools, but was not favourably impressed by them. The people are taxed to support the public schools, and miserable ones they are. One was only about seven feet high, three feet being underground and four feet above. There were no maps, charts, or other facilities for better instructing children in the school. The education is limited for the most part to reading, writing, spelling, and arithmetic. Physiology, algebra and the higher mathematics, were as unknown as political economy, or the black art of the Egyptians. The women teachers throughout the country draw salaries of from $30 to $50 per month (£6 to £10), out of which they have to pay their board ; while the male teachers are paid from $60 to $100, which is much less than the salaries paid in California, for instance. These schools are supplemented by parochial schools under the charge of the Mormons.

OF SUCH IS THE KINGDOM.

"Every woman who bears children freely is considered to be building up the Kingdom of Heaven, and they are encouraged to bring their offspring to church, whether they cry or not. It would be considered cruelty to keep them out. An article in the "Nineteenth Century" recently deplored the fact that a Fifth Avenue Church in New York with 1,500 communicants had a Sunday School of only a hundred scholars. In the district of Provo in Utah there are fully 500 children, although it is a very small place ; and if the Church referred to had scholars proportionately to those in Provo, there would have been 3,482 instead of one hundred attending the school. The Mormons think they will be gods in the other world if they are fruitful, and faithful to their creed.

UTAH'S NATURAL WEALTH.

" The Washatch range of mountains is honeycombed with silver and lead mines. The Quintah range has a great deal of gold. The steam from the hot springs along the borders of the valley is utilised to evaporate the waters of Great Salt Lake, and the salt obtained is fine in quality and unlimited in quantity. This salt is used in silver mining to separate the silver from the gold."

CALLED IT SQUARE.

Referring to the tithing system, Mr. White said he heard of a Mormon who had contributed two "balky" horses to the Church. On being informed by the receiver that they were inclined to stop suddenly, he replied : "Oh, I have eighteen more of the same sort, so I guess you are entitled to two of them ! "

Mr. White said it was quite common for the tithes to be paid in kind. " If a man could not spare the money he would, perhaps, give a sack of potatoes. Sometimes after hawking about a load of vegetables all day until they became demoralised, the conscientious Mormon would square himself with his conscience by turning his unsaleable produce over as an offering unto the cause."

WIVES AND HAIR-PULLING.

While on the way to California about two years ago, I conversed with a wealthy rancher from Idaho, a territory adjoining Utah; which is also largely peopled by Mormons, who said :—" Mormonism is not in a declining state, although the Legislature prohibits polygamous marriages. Of course the Saints' practices are not as public as they were, but still in Idaho and Utah

E

there are many men who have as many as five or six wives, and some known to me have eight or nine. I have lived among the Mormons nine years, for they run the whole country there—nearly two-thirds of the population being disciples of Brigham Young—and our relations have always been amicable ; but I could never understand their methods.

" ' How is it,' said I, to several Mormon Bishops with whom I was travelling, ' that you can keep so many wives without their indulging in hair-pulling sometimes ? '

" ' My friend,' he replied, ' if you will join our sect you will quickly discover the reason.'

" I'm not curious, and so I am still a Gentile. It is hard to determine how many of the sect really believe that an angel appeared to Joseph Smith, or who accept all the Mormon doctrines. I rather think that the license granted them has a greater attraction than anything else. Ostensibly a man is supposed to obtain his wife's consent before he can marry another woman, but if she is a ' true believer ' she does not object, and if she is not faithful to the creed, why it doesn't trouble him at all.

" Utah is trying hard to be admitted as one of the States of the Union, but the country sees plainly that although the leaders of the church profess their willingness to abandon bigamy and polygamy, it would be an easy matter for them to rescind these promises, and reinstate any of their practices without fear as soon as they are admitted to the power derived from statehood."

This latter struggle is still going on, but as yet with no satisfactory result to the Mormons.

CHAPTER VI.

"The Chamber of Torture! And the roof was made of that shape to stifle the victim's cries! . . . See the stone trough! says Goblin. For the water torture! Gurgle, swill, bloat, burst, for the Redeemer's honour! Suck the bloody rag, deep down into your unbelieving body, heretic, at every breath you draw! And when the executioner plucks it out, reeking with the smaller mysteries of God's own image, know us for his chosen servants, true believers in the Sermon on the Mount, elect disciples of Him who never did a miracle but to heal, who never struck a man with palsy, blindness, deafness, dumbness, madness, any one affliction of mankind; and never stretched His blessed hand out, but to give relief and ease."

DICKENS' "PICTURES FROM ITALY."

THE ENDOWMENT HOUSE.

SINCE my return to England the lines of the Mormons have not fallen in pleasant places, and some terrible disclosures have been made.

In November last, a Mormon named John Moore applied for admission to citizenship in view of impending municipal elections. He admitted under oath that he had been through the Endowment House, and on this ground it was contended by the Gentiles that he was not eligible to citizenship. The case was contested and a number of witnesses examined.

The Endowment House was established in order that ' Celestial marriages ' might be performed in a holy sanctuary. The house was used as a makeshift until

E 2

Joseph Smith's dream of a massive temple could be realised, where ordinances essential to the salvation of the Saints would be performed.

Mrs. Stenhouse, the wife of a Mormon elder, in her life-story "Escaped from the Mormons," states that she went through the Endowment House in Salt Lake City with her husband, and that the ceremony was the most ridiculous spectacle she ever saw. They donned white temple robes, and their eyes, ears and mouths were anointed with oil. The women were then washed all over by Mrs. Eliza R. Snow, the poetess, and Mrs. Whitney, who has published " Why we practise plural marriage," and other works. Each woman was then told the name she would bear in glory. One was deaf, and her name was spoken loud enough for others to hear. This disclosed the fact that all the women were to bear the name of Sarah in Paradise! Then a kind of sacred drama, illustrating the devil's tempting Eve to eat the forbidden fruit, was played; and Mrs. Stenhouse and her husband were sealed for time and eternity to each other, and the ordinary formula of marriage was gone through.

SWORE THEY WOULD OBEY.

But after taking the third degree the most horrible oaths were administered to those who had been initiated into the mysteries. Mrs. Stenhouse narrates what happened in the following words :—

"At this stage of our rehearsal we were taught certain passwords and grips ; then we were arranged in a circle. The women covered their faces with their veils, and we all kneeled down, and, with our right hands uplifted towards heaven, we took the solemn oath of obedience and secrecy. We vowed that by every means in our power we would seek to avenge the death of Joseph Smith, the

Prophet, upon the Gentiles who had caused his murder, and that we would teach our children to do so; we vowed that, without murmur or questioning, we would implicitly obey the commands of the priesthood in everything; we vowed that we would not commit adultery—which, with reference to the men, was explained to mean the taking of wives without the permission of the holy priesthood; and we vowed that we would never, under any circumstances, reveal that which transpired in the Endowment House.

"The penalty for breaking the oath, which was worded in the most startling and impressive way, was then explained to us. The traitor's intestines were—while he was yet living—to be torn from him, his throat was to be cut from ear to ear, and his heart and tongue were to be cut out. In the world to come, everlasting damnation would be his portion. Let not the reader think that this was merely an imaginary penalty, or that it was expressed merely for the purpose of frightening the weak-minded; for, as will be shown, punishments quite as horrible as that have been deliberately meted out to the Apostate, the Gentile, and the suspected Saint, by the Mormon priesthood. The innocent blood which cries for vengeance against Brigham Young and some of the leaders of the Church, is sufficient to weigh the purest spirit which stands before the throne of God down to the nethermost abysses of hell.

"The vow we took differed from that given in the Nauvoo Temple, and given by Van Dusen. We reproduce it here that it may be seen that although Mormonism may change in some of its details, it is, and always has been, a system on which treason, revenge, and bloodshed are included as duties; and as such are dangerous to the United States.

"We are required to kneel at the altar, where we have an oath administered, to the effect that we will henceforth and for ever, use all our influence to destroy this nation (the United States), and teach it to our posterity. We are sworn by a solemn oath, that we will never reveal to any person what we do and see in the temple. The oath is as follows: "You do solemnly swear in the presence of Almighty God, His angels, and these witnesses (pointing to individuals in the room that have secret instructions to take life) that you will, from this time henceforth and for ever, begin to carry out hostilities against this nation, and teach it to your children; and to keep the same intent a profound secret now and for ever, so help you God."

This statement does not rest on the authority of Mrs. Stenhouse alone, for many of the witnesses in the Salt Lake Court made similar disclosures.

John Bond, an apostate, said he went through the Endowment House in January, 1868, and in Room Five he took an oath to obey the priesthood in everything temporal, spiritual, political, social and financial. The penalty for violation of the oaths and divulging the oaths, was death by cutting the throat from ear to ear, and cutting out the heart and tongue, and disembowelment. He also swore to avenge Joseph Smith's death, and carry out hostilities against the United States. William Woodruff, the present President of the Mormon Church, officiated, and fifty men and women went through the ceremony on that occasion.

HAD SEEN APOSTATES SLAIN.

Martin D. Waddell, sixty-seven years old, made similar statements, adding that he saw a man named Green, who had apostatised, have his throat cut from ear to ear. He gave full details of the crime, and the names of some men who participated in that murder, who are still living.

When the witness and others remonstrated, they were told they would be served the same way if they did not keep quiet.

W. H. Dame, who was the leader of the band, said after the crime : " He apostatised once, and now he has apostatised, and gone to hell."

The witness testified that Green's property, consisting of $5,000 in cash, and a wagonload of merchandise, were taken to the church tithing yard in this city. Dame was one of the principals in the Mountain Meadow massacre.

Bishop Cahoon testified that he knew many men who had been secretly murdered by order of the Church, and gave their names. James McGuffy, another witness, seventy-five years old, connected the Mountain Meadow massacre with the oaths taken at the Endowment House. He said there were three organised bands of chief murderers in those days. They were called Danites,* Blood Atoners, and Avengers. They had the work appointed to them by Brigham Young, who was considered God on earth.

BRIGHAM AND HIS BOWIE-KNIFE.

Verbatim extracts from sermons delivered in the tabernacle were read in evidence. Brigham Young preaching on apostacy, once said " I say that rather than that apostates should flourish here, I will unsheath my bowie-knife and conquer or die." This called forth applause from the congregation. In another sermon he said " If a man needs salvation and it is necessary to spill his blood on earth in order that he may be saved,— spill it. That is the way to love mankind. I could refer you to plenty of instances where men have been righteously slain in order to atone for their sins. I have seen scores and hundreds of people for whom there would have been chances in the last resurrection, if their blood had been spilled on the ground as a smoking incense to the Almighty."

THE EXECUTIONER.

Dr. Richards, who said he belonged to the Melchizideck order of the Mormon priesthood, testified that he understood it to be a doctrine of the church that if a man apo staised he should yield himself up voluntarily to be killed for the atonement of his sin ; and he supposed

---

* The name 'Danites' was an allusion to the passage Genesis xlix, 17.

President Brigham Young would appoint an executioner. Several witnesses refused to testify, being in fear of their lives. One said his wife would be forfeited to the church. Another said an old cavalry sabre was exhibited under a peculiar light, so as to make a ghastly sight, when the oath was taken.

E. L. T. Harrison, a journalist, who had been excommunicated because he had advocated the opening of the mines, which Brigham Young did not favour, fearing it would cause an influx of Gentiles, testified that the hostility to the United States was because of the enforcement of the law against polygamy.

A MORMON NOT A CITIZEN.

The result of this evidence was that Judge Anderson decided in November 29th, 1889, that no alien who is a member of the Mormon church is a fit person to be made a citizen of the United States. Should the other Utah Judges uphold this decision, the effect on the Mormon people politically will be most disastrous. The matter has never been carried to a higher Court, and a letter from a reliable source, written in March last from Salt Lake City, informed me that as far as alien Mormons are concerned, they are still denied citizenship. The report of this decision in the San Francisco " Examiner " concludes :—

" The evidence," he says, " establishes beyond any reasonable doubt that endowment ceremonies are inconsistent with the oath of citizenship." In summing up, he says " whether the language of Brigham Young, Heber Kimball, Orson Hyde and others, instigated the Mountain Meadow massacre, or whether that horrible butchery was done by the direct command of Brigham Young, will probably never be known.

"The evidence," Judge Anderson says, "does not sustain the claim of the counsel that the feelings of the people toward the Government have undergone a change, and that in later years the feeling of hostility has disappeared or become greatly modified. On the contrary, the evidence showed that the people have persistently refused obedience to at least a portion of the laws of this Government, and have insulted and driven the United States officers from the Territory, and denied the authority of the United States to pass laws prohibiting polygamy ; as unwarranted interference with the Mormon religion." He closes by saying : — " The evidence in this case establishes, unquestionably, that the teachings, and practices, and purposes of the Mormon Church are antagonistic to the Government of the United States ; and are utterly subversive of good morals and the well-being of society, and that its members are animated by feelings of hostility toward the Government and its laws ; therefore, an alien who is a member of said church is not a fit person to be made a citizen of the United States."

"Nothing that has ever happened to the Mormon Church has thrown its adherents into such a state of despondency and shame."

NOT AN UNPARDONABLE SIN.

Mrs. Stenhouse says that the murder of a Gentile was never considered by the Church to be an absolutely unpardonable sin ; but the shedding of innocent blood (*i.e.*, killing a Mormon) could only be expiated by the death of the murderer. A woman came to her one night and said that a band of masked men had taken her husband out; and subsequently brought back his body with the throat cut from ear to ear. They threatened to treat her in the same way if she revealed this blood-atonement of an apostate.

In 1878 Orrin Porter Rockwell died. He was said to be the chief of the band of Destroying Angels or Danites, and to have slain over a hundred apostates with his own hand.

CHAPTER VII.

I am Demon Revenge, and with glee I cry
   'A tooth for a tooth, and an eye for an eye;
A life for a life, and a soul for a soul,'
   For my devilish wrath is like blazing coal;
And my thirst for blood is only quenched
   When limb from limb is asunder wrenched!
A hundred lives I would have for one,
   And torturing foes is infernal fun!

*   *   *   *   *   *   *

Lo, the blood of the innocent crieth,
   And conjureth visions of hell,
Where the murderer's soul ever lieth,
   Mid flames and sulphurous smell!
In torment the slayer will languish
   As eternity's Pendulum swings,
And death would be sweet to the anguish
   Each hour to the damn'd mortal brings!

MOUNTAIN MEADOW MASSACRE.

THE blackest page in the history of Mormonism is the Mountain Meadow massacre—a page which can never be obliterated from the memories of the American people. But in considering this horrible outrage, it must not be forgotten that the rank and file of the Mormons were not responsible for its perpetration. We must endeavour to fasten the guilt on the right shoulders, or at any rate refrain from condemning deluded and fanatical people who were merely tools in the hands of wicked men.

There would have been more excuse for the actual murderers, perhaps, if it had been a religious extermination, although even then the apologist would have a most difficult task before him. The bloody wars engaged in by religious zealots afford a favourite theme for denunciation, to the free-thinker ; and probably have done more to embitter the feelings of the latter class to the religionists than anything else. Paine, Ingersoll, and others who have attacked historical christianity, have seized upon Jewish massacres, which were said to have been ordered by God, and they have raised strong doubts as to the divine sanction.

THE DESTRUCTION OF JERICHO.

We are told in the book of Joshua (6th chapter) that when the Israelites passed over Jordan into Canaan and surrounded the city of Jericho, the priests blew trumpets and the people shouted, and the walls of Jericho fell down flat, "so that the people went up into the city, every man straight before him, and they took the city. And they utterly destroyed all that was in the city, both man and woman, young and old, and ox, and sheep, and ass, with the edge of the sword."

It is intimated that this was required as the city was accursed, and the people were so wicked that extermination was necessary.

But we have vile people existing in the world to-day. Suppose the Mormons, the Fire-Worshippers, the Red Indian or the English Protestant of to-day, claimed to have been inspired to inaugurate an onslaught on the dwellers in the slums of our cities or the aristocratic lepers in our palaces ; who would believe them, or admit their right to slaughter these people, bad as they may be ? There is not a rational man who does not revolt at the tortures to which religious bigots have often subjected unbelievers during the horrors of the Inquisition ; the War of the Crusades ; or the persecution of any sect by a stronger hierarchy, such as we know has ofttimes taken place in England in the past.

HISTORY REPEATS ITSELF.

Yet in spite of our conviction that God will not authorise one body of men to slay another portion of the community in our own day ; and that the gallows would probably be meted out to those who had such sanguinary revelations, and tried to realise them ; we know well that so-called ' religious history ' is replete with episodes of this character.

I make these remarks because mauy Protestants, Romanists, and others who may chance to glance at the particulars of the Mountain Meadow massacre which follow, may without reading further, turn away in righteous horror, ready to condemn *in toto* the Mormon creed as inhuman, and every individual believer in Mormonism as a blood-thirsty villain.

Judgment must be exercised in this matter as in the study of the Scriptures. If the christian religion were to be held responsible for all the crimes that have been perpetrated in its name, few would go to it for the guiding rules of life. I question if many large bodies of professed believers in religious doctrines can be found, whose history has not been smirched with many a bloody stain of intolerance and crime. So the fact that the Mormon Church has this great Massacre to answer for, does not prove it worse, as a whole, than other organised churches. Our more humane and logical view of the matter is to condemn only the few instigators of the fiendish butchery.

REVENGE, THE MOTIVE POWER.

According to the testimony of the witnesses previously quoted, the Mormon Church would not scruple to justify the Mountain Meadow massacre on fanatical religious grounds among themselves; but, viewing the matter objectively, the deed was utterly unjustifiable, and was the outcome of a desire for revenge. Subsequent developments showed the leading men of the church that their wisest course was to feign ignorance of the occurrence, rather than attempt to palliate the offence by any explanation based on religious reasons. The narrative shows there were no extenuating circumstances, and the guilty parties merited the most extreme punishment.

THE HORROR DESCRIBED.

Mrs. Stenhouse says the Mountain Meadow massacre occurred early in September, 1857. About one hundred and twenty or thirty emigrants from Arkansas were proceeding in waggons through Utah, and camped at Jordan river to rest, and lay in fresh supplies; but they were boycotted by order of Brigham Young, because Parley P. Pratt, a Mormon writer, had been killed in Arkansas by a man named McLean, because Pratt had run away with, and married McLean's wife.

The Mormon theory was that as the Arkansas people had sided with McLean, they were the enemies of the the Latter Day Saints.

After they had moved on the order was given by Brigham Young that they should be followed. Brigham was at that time Governor of Utah, Commander-in-Chief of Militia, and Indian agent as well, so he was responsible for the commission of crime, or at any-rate for the punishment of all offenders that came under his jurisdiction. The Mormon militia disguised themselves as Red Indians, and, together with a number of Indians, rode after the emigrant train. Major John D. Lee was commander of the militia, and was accompanied by President Haight and other authorities of the church in Southern Utah. They came up in several companies, the Mormons pretending to be friends of the emigrants, whom they induced to lay down arms and retrace their steps towards Salt Lake City, promising them defence from the hostile Indians.

DECOYED, SURROUNDED, AND BUTCHERED.

The emigrants, believing their promises and representations, were decoyed, some distance, and then the Indians and disguised Mormons fell upon the band and massacred the men, women, and youths, saving only children too young to remember the occurrence. Young girls were chased and ruthlessly shot down, and the wolves soon feasted on their remains. Jewellery torn from the mangled bodies of women was worn publicly on the streets in Salt Lake City afterwards, and clothes of the murdered men were found in the store house.

BRIGHAM WAS SILENT.

It is a singular fact that Brigham Young made no

report at headquarters of the massacre, and took no steps to bring the perpetrators to justice. Twenty years later, however, after the death of other parties connected with the massacre, he allowed Elder Lee to be tried and convicted; and Lee was sentenced to be shot on the scene of the slaughter.

Before he was riddled with bullets he said :—" I did my utmost to save those people, and I am sacrificed for others. I believe that Brigham Young is trying to mislead the people." He made other remarks, in which he said his conscience was easy, his belief in the divine mission of Joseph Smith as strong as ever, and he believed he should go to Heaven. He mentioned three of his numerous wives, to whom he desired photographs of himself—taken at the scene of the execution—should be given.

Such is a synopsis of the story of this massacre as described in Mrs. Stenhouse's work. She says that at the present time there are many murderers walking the streets of Salt Lake City who are known to have taken part in it.

TALMAGE ON THE MASSACRE.

The Rev. T. De Witt Talmage, D.D., in his sermon on " Mormonism : an Exposure " gives a vivid account of the massacre, in which the details are somewhat different to the foregoing. The orator thus eloquently discants on the horrors of that awful event :—

" In 1857, a company of emigrants started from Arkansas and Missouri for California. They were good, respectable, well-to-do people ; but they had an idea that they might have larger comforts for their families on the other side the mountains ; so they undertook, what always seems to be a terrible thing, travelling in the waggon emigrant train. They suffered everything on the way. By night the fires kept off the wolves, and by day there was fatigue and hunger, and heat, and gentle womanhood fainting with the long journey, and children crying for food. There were one hundred and seventy in that company.

"They must needs cross Utah territory, and in Utah nearly all the emigrant trains were accustomed to take in new supplies of provisions; but Brigham Young heard that this emigrant train was coming, and he forbade, under pain of death, any Mormon in Utah giving any clothing, or food, or medicine, or kindness of any sort, to these emigrants. It was a revenge for the fact that a man in Arkansas had slain Elder Pratt, of the Mormon Church, because he (Elder Pratt) had stolen the wife of the man in Arkansas, and taken her to Utah, and into Mormonism.

"On and on went this emigrant train, suffering all indignity, until they came to a plain called Mountain Meadow. The Indians dashed down upon the emigrants, but they threw up a barricade, and in this temporary fortress drove back the red men most successfully. Then the Mormon militia dashed down upon them; but you know how men will fight when they fight for their wives and children, and so the Mormon militia were driven back.

SHOOTING LITTLE GIRLS.

"Still, it was only with great peril that anyone could leave the temporary fortress, even to get water from the spring near by. There was great suffering from thirst;

F

so one day they despatched two little girls, clad in white, to bring water from the spring. They said, 'Most certainly the Mormon militia will not disturb them;' but no sooner had they appeared outside the barricade, than they were shot dead.

"Petitions for relief were signed by all the emigrants, and by Oddfellows and Freemasons, who made appeals to members of their particular order. Three brave men volunteered to carry that petition for relief to California. An aged Methodist minister of the group, in prayer, commended these three men to God, and the emigrants all knelt in supplication; but hardly had these three brave men started on their journey than they were butchered.

"Time passed on, and one day waggons were seen coming. 'Now,' thought the poor emigrants, 'we shall have relief,' and they could not restrain their glee at the thought of liberation. The waggons came up, and from them came a flag of truce, saying, 'If you emigrants will surrender, and put down your arms, you may walk out into perfect liberty, and you shall not be harmed.' Thinking the proposition a fair one, it was accepted, and they put down their arms, according to the arrangement, and then the men marched out first, then came the women, and then came the children. After they were outside the barricade, the Mormon militia, with guns and knives and daggers, massacred all save a few little children, whom they thought to be too young to tell the story. Aged and young husbands, and wives, parents and children, left dead on the plain! Women belonging to the emigrant train, who were sick and unable to walk, were then taken out by the Mormons into the presence of their murdered families, stripped of their clothing, shot dead, and hurled upon the heap of corpses.

HER MOTHER'S DRESS.

" The waggons, the stock of the train, the dresses of the women, and their jewellery, amounting in all to a property of $300,000, taken possession of by the Mormon Government. Years after, a Mormon woman, showing a silk dress that had been captured from the train—showing one of these silk dresses in Salt Lake City—one of the little girls that had been saved from the massacre recognised it. She said, ' Oh ! that's my mother's. Where's mamma ? Why don't mamma come ? Mamma used to wear that ! ' And she burst into tears.

"John D. Lee, the Mormon Bishop, was the presiding spirit in person of the massacre; and when, fifteen or eighteen years after, in the court-room, he gave testimony, he said he had orders to do that from head-quarters ; and it appeared on the evidence that Brigham Young had given orders as to the disposition of the property of these murdered people, and had told the witnesses to hush up; and all Christendom to-day holds that man responsible for the tragedy. No wonder, when years after he visited the scene, and found that the bones of the emigrants had been decently buried by the officers of the United States Government, and General Carlton had put up a head-board by the grave, with— for an epitaph—the inscription, " Vengeance is Mine : I will repay, saith the Lord "—no wonder that Brigham Young, seeing that inscription, ordered it to be torn down.

SULPHUROUS LANGUAGE.

" It is the presiding spirit of the Mountain Meadow

massacre that I arraign to-day for trial before you, the jury of Americans. It still lives. It has its throne in Salt Lake City ; and its foot on the heart of dishonoured women, and its breath is the pestilence of the nation. Gory, ghastly, hideous, infernal Mormonism, stand up and look into the faces of the American jury that is to try you."

RAIL ROAD NEWS DEPOT
PAPERS MAGAZINES AMERICANS,
FOREIGN PERIODICALS BOOKS STATIONERY

CHAPTER VIII.

"But the fearful and unbelieving, and the abominable and murderers, and whoremongers, and sorcerers, and idolaters, and all liars, shall have their part in the lake which burneth with fire and brimstone: which is the second death."

Revelation xxi. 8.

"Snatch from His hand the balance and the rod,
Rejudge His justice, be the god of God."

POPE'S "ESSAY ON MAN."

HORRIBLE DOCTRINES AND DEEDS.

IN the course of her sketchy and stirring (but somewhat rambling) story, Mrs. Stenhouse makes a good many strong assertions, many of which naturally rest on her veracity. For instance she says:—"Certain sins cannot be forgiven here on earth—shedding Mormon blood, divulging the secrets of the Endowment House, marital unfaithfulness on the part of the wife, or apostacy; these are unpardonable. All other crimes which Gentiles abhor may become even virtues, if done in the cause of the Church. I do not, of course, mean to say that the mass of the Mormon people act up to such atrocious doctrines; for although, when among themselves, they would admit that the theory was correct, the better instincts of their nature keep them from ever putting that theory into practice. But what I do mean to say is, that such doctrines have, over and over again, been distinctly taught in the plainest words in the public hearing of thousands; that they have been printed and reprinted by authority; and have been practised, and the very highest of the Mormon leaders have applauded ; and that, even at the present moment, these doctrines form part of the dogmas of the Church. It is this day a matter of fact, and not a matter of question, that if any Mormon apostate were to commit any of the unpardonable sins which I have mentioned, and if he or she were to be assassinated by a private individual, all zealous Mormons would maintain that not only was the deed justifiable, but even meritorious !"

She charges Joseph Smith with prophesying in 1841 that Boggs, ex-Governor of Missouri, would die by violent hands within a year; and that afterwards he offered 500 dollars to several Danites (i.e., the army of Zion) to assassinate him. Boggs was severely wounded, but not killed; and Smith said of some of the Danites who were missing about this time, that they had gone to prophesy.

Another of her assertions is that in 1866, O. N. Brassfield, a Gentile, who married the second wife of an elder, was assassinated; and the report was circulated that he had gone to Europe on a mission.

In October, 1866, Dr. J. King Robinson, a Gentile, who had married the daughter of a Mormon widow, who had seceded from the church, was also mysteriously murdered.

THE HAND-CART SCHEME.

Mrs. Stenhouse accuses the heads of the early Mormon Church of reckless disregard of the lives of believers, in connection with the " Hand-cart Scheme." Converts from Europe and the Eastern States of America were ordered to proceed across the Continent in mid-winter, and told that God would take them safe through and preserve them amid all the dangers of the journey. Captains of hundreds and fifties were chosen, and each emigrant had one hundred pounds weight of luggage.

DIED ON THE WAY.

Mrs. Stenhouse and her husband, who was a New York journalist, started with a hand-cart company in mid-winter—February, 1846, from New York. The pilgrimage was almost a repetition of the wanderings of the children of Israel in the wilderness. They were smitten with plague, frozen with cold, suffered from hunger, sank by the wayside exhausted, and hundreds died by the way. Young girls and old women dragged along their carts, buoyed up with faith that they would soon reach the earthly Zion, until compelled to give up the struggle and die. The atmosphere when they camped was intolerable, and the sights indescribable ; as many were too weak to preserve the decencies of civilisation. Bodies would be found in the morning with marks of wolf-fangs on them.

She heard that women and children were whipped to make them keep up, and to keep life in them. " I did not see this myself," says she, " but I believe if the story was true it was an act of mercy, and not of cruelty."

TALMAGE ON THE WAR-PATH.

But strong as are the denunciations of the Elder's wife, they are as gentle chidings compared with the hail-storm of sweeping conclusions drawn by Dr. Talmage. He charges ' Mormonism ' with almost every crime he can call to mind. But what does he mean by Mormonism? The people's lives may be pure and their creed impure; or the creed may be good and the lives of its professors vile; or the lives of the bulk of the people may be superior to those of the heads of the church; or the Mormons as a whole may be mistaken, but conscientious.

This is what he says:—

" I charge Mormonism with being one great and prolonged cruelty. Nobody denies the work of the destroying angels called Danites, whose chief business it was to hunt up antagonism to the Mormon Government, and put it to death. It was for years the land of assassination, and the field of blood. No one doubts the Hickman butcheries under Brigham Young. I saw a cellar where a mother and two sons had been put to death— the mother slain in the presence of her sons, and the two sons butchered, because they had revealed the secrets of the Mormon Government. The whole world has heard the story of the destruction of the Aiken party. And these Mormons have a delicious vernacular by which they describe this putting to death. They say all these things with a smile and a jeer. 'Oh, they were put out of the way,' or 'they met with a bad accident,' or 'they were used up,' or 'they were cut off just under their ears!'

" Why have these atrocities stopped? Because a regiment of United States soldiers are on the hill overlooking the city, and with iron rake of destruction may rake that city if it attempts to repeat such atrocity. It is not because Mormonism is more merciful, but because it has not the courage.

BRIGHAM'S BLASPHEMY.

" I charge Mormonism with being a great blasphemy. Brigham Young, in one of his sermons, declared that Christ himself was a practical polygamist ; that Mary and Martha were His plural wives; that Mary Magdalene was another ; and he said in the same sermon that the bridal feast in Cana of Galilee, where Christ turned water into wine, was the occasion of one of His own marriages ! The whole tendency of the system is towards blasphemy. I was told over and over again that Brigham Young, with slight provocation, would swear like a fishwoman at Billingsgate.

" I charge upon Mormonism that it is a disloyalty to the United States Government. There is an oath taken in the Endowment House at Salt Lake City, which subverts all other oaths. Perjury is no crime when enacted in behalf of Mormonism. Mormonisn hates the Government of the United States with a perfect hatred. Fourth of July, and all patriotic demonstrations, are an utter abhorrence to the Mormons ; and the Gentile celebrators of the fourth of July suffer every indignity. Mormonism would like the United States Government to perish to-day.

" *I charge upon Mormonism that it is an organised filth built on polygamy.* There is a man in Salt Lake City who has three wives, and they are the mother, the grand-mother, and the grand-daughter.

" I tell you Mormonism is one great surge of licentiousness ; it is the seraglio of the Republic, it is the concentrated corruption of this land, it is the brothel of the nation, it is hell enthroned.

PHYSICAL FORCE.

" If the Mormons submit to the law, all right. If not, then send out troops of the United States Government, and let them make the Mormon Tabernacle their headquarters, and with cannon of the biggest bore thunder into them the seventh commandment. Arbitration by all means; but if that will not do, then peaceful proclamation. If that will not do, then howitzer, and bombshell, and bullets, and cannon-ball.

" I make no war against Mormonism as a religion. I war against Mormonism as an immorality, as a defiance of civil law, as an institution Anti-American. When Brigham Young's men, with bowie-knives, broke up Judge Drummond's court in 1856, and compelled him to adjourn it *sine die*; and when Mormonism poised loose rocks on the top of cliffs, where you may see them to this day, expecting to throw them over on the United States troops as they passed under, Mormonism showed what she thought of our Government.'

" Now, as I have impanelled you as a jury to sit in trial of this giant of lust and disloyalty, and the evidence has been presented before you, are you ready for the verdict before you leave the jury-box ? Guilty, or not guilty ? "Guilty," says one. " Guilty," say all.

MORMONISM ON THE GALLOWS.

" Then, what shall the sentence be ? It must not be a small incarceration, it must not be a slight censure. While we have only pity for the victims of this abomination, and we pray God He will speedily deliver them ; for this institution of Mormonism, as such, only extinction and death. But where shall be the execution, and when shall the execution take place? What scaffolding will be strong enough to hold such a monster of iniquity? One end of the scaffolding must be planted on the Rocky Mountains, and the other on the Sierra Nevadas. But what Friday, of what gloomy week, of what gloomy month, of what gloomy year, would be gloomy enough for the execution of this beastly outlaw? What grave deep enough for this stout, thousand-armed, thousand-footed, thousand-headed, thousand-horned, thousand-fanged corpse? What epitaph for that grave unless it be this :—

"Here lies Mormonism, the outlaw, the libertine, and the murderer—the hero of Mountain Meadow massacre. Born February, 22, 1827. Died 1882, at the hand of the law, and under the instruction of the Almighty. 'Then the Lord rained upon Sodom brimstone and fire from the Lord out of heaven.'"

A PERORATION.

" I plead for womanhood in Utah—womanhood under foot, womanhood in the sewer, womanhood crushed until it cannot weep, womanhood looking out of the barred windows of a perdition of anguish towards what seems an unpitying heaven, crying " O Lord! how long, O Lord ? "—womanhood in the pandemonium of a polygamous home—womanhood with the garlands of hope and affection and honour, torn with the swine's snout of incestuous abomination—womanhood that, if it had a chance, or had had a chance in the past, would have been as pure and good as that which presides at your table to-day, or which long ago bent in benediction over your peaceful cradle, before you began the struggle with the world.

" O men, with wives and daughters, and mothers;
O brothers, with sisters! Do not your ears tingle, and
does not your blood run cold, at this story of Mormonism? And are you not determined at the ballot-box,
and with pen and tongue, and in every possible way, to
war against it ?"

CHAPTER IX.

"O sorrowing women, ye who weep in vain,
Who uncaressed, sob on through the dark night,
With broken wings that ache to feel the light,
    Strained out above joy's corpse untimely slain—

*　　*　　*　　*　　*

O hearts forsaken, hearts forlorn, oppressed,
My arms are strong, my breast is warm and true ;
Here is sweet love if love ye never knew,
    Here dear unquestioning sympathy, here rest."

AMELIE RIVES.

THE GREEN-EYED MONSTER.

M RS. Joseph Cook, in "Face to Face with Mormonism," cites the case of a mother who said of her
dead child " Every hour of its little life it shed tears
that I repressed before its birth, and the agony that I
hid in my heart killed it at last."

Mrs. Stenhouse never seems to have believed in the
divine origin of the re-institution of polygamy, so her
experience would not be a criterion of the feelings
of Mormon women who believe that they are doing
right, and who cheerfully carry the teaching of
Joseph Smith into effect. Mrs. Stenhouse's husband
started the first daily paper in Salt Lake City, " The
Daily Telegraph," and when it prospered, thought it
was time to take another wife and get more glory. A
girl named Carrie was in love with him, but she died
after confessing her secret to his wife.

HE MARRIED BELINDA.

Stenhouse then courted Belinda, daughter of Parley P. Pratt, and wanted his wife's consent to his marriage with her. Mrs. Stenhouse tells how she hated the sight of the girl, but she believed that her husband's eternal welfare must first be considered, so after much agony she gave her consent.

The ceremony was performed in the Endowment House, the first wife placing Miss Pratt's hand in that of her husband as a sign that the three were then united. Mr. Stenhouse was also again married to his first wife, by proxy for Carrie, the dead girl, who was thus 'sealed' to him for eternity. Brigham Young himself performed the ceremony. She then tells how jealousy possessed her ; and she did not believe that God ever intended her husband to live with another woman.

She virtually admits that many of the Mormon men do not really believe that they do wrong, or that their wives are unhappy, for she says :—

" How terribly these Mormon men deceive themselves ! When peace, or rather quiet, reigns in their homes they think that the spirit of God is there. But it is not so. It is a calm not like the gentle silence of sleep, but as the painful stillness of death—the death of the heart's best affections, and all that is worth calling love."

She also speaks of many Mormon ladies who confessed to her that they shared her sentiments, while others, on the contrary, seemed to fervently believe that they were doing God's will and appeared to be happy. Some Mormon women were driven by their acute sufferings to commit suicide.

BALL-ROOM SCENES.

She hated the ball-rooms, where husbands often danced with the young wives, and the old ones had to look on and wear smiling faces. She has heard women mutter " I'll be even with him yet " as some energetic elder led forth a blushing maid and neglected his first, second, third or even fourth wife. Heber C. Kimball once introduced her to five of his wives at a ball. She asked him if they were all.

" No," said he, " I have forty more scattered over the earth, but I have never seen them since they were sealed to me at Nauvoo, and I hope I never shall again."

NO MORE SCRATCHING.

If what she says is true, Brigham himself had a taste of matrimonial troubles, for he once said, " I will not stand any more of this fighting and scratching around me."

Men sometimes married sisters, and one man married a widow and her children, so it is little to be wondered at that there were stormy scenes in some of the households. The houses, in many instances, were merely huts; and when a poor man took an extra wife he merely added a little room to his house, or put his new wife in a horse-box until he accomplished this work. What was more probable, says Mrs. Stenhouse, is that he put one of his old wives in the horse-box and installed his new flame in one of the bedrooms. Brigham's idea was that men were all boys until they were a hundred years old ; and he approved of old men marrying young girls.

Charles Ellis, writing on " The Iniquities of Polygamy," gives the following interesting instances of evil in Mormon marriages :—

" Years and years ago a bright and beautiful woman, the wife of one of Boston's most honoured men, and the mother of his children, became a convert to Mormonism. One night she dressed her youngest child, a lovely little girl, in boy's clothes to disguise her, and in the darkness ran away from her home and family to join a party of Mormons going west. She went to Nauvoo, and became one of the polygamous wives of Joseph Smith. When Smith was killed this woman was sealed to Brigham Young, and lived among his wives until her death in Salt Lake a few years ago. The child, who was carried away from its father by this woman, grew up with the children of Brigham Young, and when she was a girl of sixteen was sealed to one of Brigham's sons. She had married her own brother, so to speak. A son of the wife (the Boston wife, who had deserted her husband and home to become the plural wife of Smith and Young) became a Mormon also. He married, or was sealed to, a Mormon woman. In a few months she refused to live with him. Subsequently she became a mother. When her child, a daughter, was eight years old, the mother, no divorce being granted, was sealed to Brigham Young. Eight years later her daughter was sealed to Brigham's son. Thus Brigham Young was sealed first to the runaway Boston wife ; later he was sealed to the wife of his own wife's son. Later still, Brigham's son married a girl who was the daughter of one of his father's wives, and grand-daughter of another.

G

EVIL EFFECTS OF POLYGAMY.

" This mixing up of people in polygamy has had a somewhat demoralising effect on social relations in Utah generally. There has been so much talk about the iniquity of polygamy among those who have been with honest purpose trying to break it down, that they have become too familiar with the vice they condemn in that system. It is not pleasant to hear women talking about the inwardness of polygamy in Salt Lake. They detail its horrors with a thoroughness that seems to indicate a morbid state of mind induced by constant dwelling on the subject. Men who know about such things say that there is more wickedness in Salt Lake than in most places of its size, and that there are more questionable characters in proportion to numbers among those outside of the Mormon church than there are in it. It is not surprising, perhaps, that it should be so ; for it has long been understood that one of the strongest inducements to good, or to bad conduct is familiarity with the one or the other. It would be better to ignore the evils of polygamy than to denounce them ; to kill them by developing something better in their stead than to fix them in the minds of the young by constant exposure."

I question if silence respecting evil is at all expedient. As we have seen, Mormonism is not in a decaying state, and will not be while missionaries are promulgating its doctrines in different parts of the world. At a recent convention of Mormons in Iowa, Joseph Smith, son of the founder of Mormonism, read the annual report, showing that there had been two thousand accessions to the Church during the past year. The more light that can be shed on social questions, the greater is the probability that the evil will be expurgated, provided the subjects are not treated in a jocular manner.

There is, however, a danger that too sweeping conclusions will be drawn from these instances of

MATRIMONIAL FAILURES.

If we were to investigate the state of society in any nation under the sun we should find numberless instances of matrimonial misery, dissension and oppression. The animated discussion called forth by the propounding of the question " Is marriage a failure? " by Mrs. Mona Caird, brought this fact prominently to the notice of the British public, and caused hundreds of instances of monogamous marriages, which had proved dismal failures, to be revealed. The fact, therefore, that under the Mormon system we find similar cases, must not surprise us ; nor does this in itself call for an unqualified condemnation of the whole system, or the denunciation of those who conscientiously believe in the doctrines of the Church, and live up to the established standard of morality in Mormondom.

If those who enter upon marriage lack the qualities of mind and heart which would enable them to move through life without friction, unpleasantness and unhappiness will be the inevitable result. Certain conditions, of course, will intensify the connubial discord, but a good system will not necessarily produce happiness if there is no affinity between those whose lives are legally linked together ; and on the other hand we might feel conscientiously compelled to condemn a certain course of conduct pursued by any given community, while the individuals in that community *might* be as happy, or happier, in their own line of life than they would be if a different and, on the whole, higher standard of morality were to be established in their midst in opposition to their convictions.

GOOD AND BAD EVERYWHERE.

For instance, there would be no difficulty in picking out a Mormon family, say of a husband, five wives, and fifteen children (if polygamy were not made a criminal offence) who would be happier and purer in heart than many families living under a monogamous system of marriage. The tables could also be reversed, and instances adduced in which a given family living in conformity with the " one man, one wife " standard, upheld in Engand, would be immeasurably superior to *some* Mormon families, in every sense of the term.

Therefore, isolated examples prove but little. While human nature remains as it is, there will be varieties of temperament, intellect, and moral discernment, which will produce inequalities of happiness and domestic harmony, and violations of that which is good.

What do I mean by that? I mean that no system that can ever be devised will produce a perfect working society, free from jealousies, strife, and selfish indulgence, unless the heart of man ceases to be " deceitful above all things and desperately wicked." If you blame Mormonism because of the wrecks that strew its shores, blame also the systems which are marked by similar disasters in England, France, and other parts of America, where divorces, suicides, murders, and desertions show that monogamy may give birth to evil as well as polygamy.

"But," say you, "is it not a fact that if in England there are thousands who feel, from personal experience, that monogamous marriage is a failure, it is because they are not adapted to each other, or wilfully violate the conditions which would enable them to live happily together?"

BEST TYPES OF MORMONS.

But this is the very position I take on the subject of Mormon marriages. I see no reason to believe that there is a greater amount of unhappiness or filth among the best types of Mormons who have practised plural marriage, than among the best types who believe that one man should have only one wife, and who abide by the belief. It is those who are not adapted to Mormonism whose lives are marked by marital infelicity.

This is vastly different, however, to saying that monogamy is *not* on the whole preferable to polygamy.

It is necessary to make these distinctions because careless thinkers are apt to confuse cause and effect. They see only good in their own established code of morality, and only evil in others. If a Mormon ill-treats his wife, then they hold polygamy responsible. If an Englishman or a Parisian is guilty of even greater cruelty to his spouse they blame the individual, not monogamy. This is manifestly unfair, and in my capacity of counsel for both plaintiff and defendant, I am bound to point this out. Many of the cases of conjugal infelicity in Mormondom are due solely to the fact that those who entered into polygamous marriages were weak-minded people who voluntarily agreed to share the affections of their common husband, and yet were unprepared with sufficient faith to endure heartburns which could not fail to follow, unless jealousy was cloaked with the mantle of love, self-sacrifice, and unwavering faith in the truth of that, as well as other, features of their religion.

MORE MISERY THAN HAPPINESS.

It is extremely difficult to discover whether there has been a preponderance of infelicitous Mormon marriages. If so, it would not prove that Mormonism is ' an organised filth,' as Talmage affirms, but that the bulk of the people have not been firm believers in the heavenly origin of polygamy, or acted at first on fanatical impulse, until natural passions or former prejudices re-asserted themselves.

This is what Artemus Ward says of the Mormon women :—

" Are the Mormon women happy ?

" I give it up. I don't know.

" I saw them at their best, of course—at balls, tea-parties, and the like. They were like other women, as far as my observation extended. They were hooped, and furbelowed, and shod, and white-collared, and bejewelled ; and like women all over the world, they were softer-eyed and kinder-hearted than men can ever hope to be.

THEY LOVE.

" The Mormon girl is reared to believe that the plurality wife system (as it is delicately called here) is strictly right ; and in linking her destiny with a man who has twelve wives, she undoubtedly considers she is doing her duty. She loves the man, probably, for I think it is not true, as so many writers have stated, that girls are forced to marry whomsoever "the Church" may dictate. Some parents no doubt advise, connive, threaten, and in aggravated cases incarcerate here, as some parents have always done elsewhere, and always will do as long as petticoats continue to be an institution.

A HAPPY UNION.

"I had a man pointed out to me who married an entire family. He had originally intended to marry Jane, but Jane did not want to leave her widowed mother. The other three sisters were not in the matrimonial market for the same reason; so this gallant man married the whole crowd, including the girl's grandmother, who had lost all her teeth, and had to be fed with a spoon. The family were in indigent circumstances, and they could not but congratulate themselves on securing a wealthy husband. It seemed to affect the grandmother deeply, for the first words she said on reaching her new home were, ' Now thank God! I shall have my gruel reg'lar!'"

CHAPTER X.

"This scene is my delight, for here
Are devils mixed with true believers."

GOETHE'S "FAUST."

BRIGHAM'S CHARACTER.

MRS. Stenhouse is unsparing in her denunciation of Brigham Young. She says he looked like a retired sea-captain. He was remorseless. He connived at, if not suggested, some of the most atrocious crimes ever perpetrated on the face of the earth. His favourite wife was Amelia Folsom Young, and she was his master, so he was under petticoat government at last.

W. F. Rae had written of him as the embodiment of avarice and lust. He was mean, and had cheated her out of money for some bonnets she sold his wives. Men were paid in Salt Lake notes, which were current only in Utah Territory, and they had not handled United States coin for years, so could not leave the Mormon community if they desired. A large sum of money had been collected to build the temple, and millions of dollars raised by tithing and other means; but during Brigham's lifetime no one had sufficient courage to demand an account of those funds, and the interest and compound interest which should be accruing thereto.

Brigham intended to proclaim himself King, and declare his independence of the United States. He was in the habit of borrowing large sums of money from the Church, and squaring the account by turning in a bill for 'services rendered.' He kept the money of converts who travelled to Zion under the hand-cart scheme. Brigham misled press men and authors generally who came to Salt Lake City, by treating them well, and showing them the bright side of everything through a pair of Mormon spectacles.

BELINDA WAS DIVORCED.

The history of Mrs. Stenhouse showed that her family had no reason to bless Brigham. When the Prophet began to run things with a high hand, and desired to get control of all the industries, he was strongly opposed by a Gentile paper. Mr. Stenhouse's paper was neutral, so Brigham conceived the idea that the "Daily Telegraph" was not his friend, and ordered Stenhouse to move his paper to Ogden, promising that it should be a success.

Belinda Pratt, meanwhile, had secured a divorce from Stenhouse, who then considered the advisability of marrying Zina Young, one of Brigham Young's daughters.

Mrs. Stenhouse's daughter, Clara, married Joseph A. Young, one of the prophet's sons. As Mr. Stenhouse still retained some amount of faith in the "revelator," he obeyed his commands and his paper collapsed. Subsequently he apostatised; his wife and himself resigned their positions in the Church; and afterwards made a living by journalism in the eastern States.

POLYTHEISM: ADAM A GOD.

Mrs. Stenhouse is right when she says that the popular idea of the Mormon faith is that except as regards polygamy it differs very little from Christianity. But she goes on to show that many of the heads of the Church have advocated entirely different views. They believed in Polytheism, saying that Joseph Smith was with the 'gods.' They did not greatly differ from Spiritualists, as they believed in three stages of progressiveness after death. Their bodies would be resurrected, but not their blood, as this, being the principle of corrupt life, would be supplanted by some other spirit.

Brigham believed that Adam was a god. Joseph Smith thought that the North American Indians were a remnant of Israel. Some Mormons were baptised for Queen Anne, King George, etc., as they considered they could act as proxies for these royal sinners.

EX-COMMUNICATED.

These and other startling views must have caused withdrawals from the British Church. According to the report for the half-year ending June 30, 1853, 11,776 persons were ex-communicated, the great cause of this relapse having been the advocacy of the doctrine of polygamy.

The following are interesting specimens of the opinions of one of Brigham's right hand-men, and of the prophet himself. Mrs. Stenhouse says :—

"Here is a bit from one of the sermons of Heber C. Kimball, which I think I must give for the reader's benefit.

"Fancy an 'Apostle!' thus addressing a large and mixed congregation of men, women, and children :—

"'Here are some edicated men jest under my nose. They come here and they think they know more than I do, and then they git the big head, and it swells and swells until it gits like the old woman's squash—you go to touch it and it goes kersmash ; and when you look for the man, why it ain't thar. They're jest like so many pots in a furnace—yer know I've been a potter in my time—

almighty thin and almighty big; and when they're sot up the heat
makes 'em smoke a little, and then they collapse and tumble in, and
they ain't no whar.' This was Heber's style in general. Next to
making modest people blush, nothing pleased him better than to
annoy or ridicule any one who had the smallest pretentions to
education; and yet naturally Heber was a kind-hearted man.

"Brigham's style was very little better, and the substance of his
discourses quite as bad.

"The Apostle Orson Pratt was the only one who dared, in the
presence of Brigham, to say that education was a proper thing, and
that there were many books which would be of good service to the
Saints, if they obtained and studied them. On one occasion
Brigham arose in ire, and said, 'The professor has told you that
there are many books in the world, and I tell you that
there are many people there. He says there is something in all
these books; I say each of those persons has got a name. It would
do you just as much good to learn those somebodies' names as it
would to read those books. Five minutes' revelation would teach
me more truth than all this pack of nonsense that I should have
packed away in my unlucky brains from books.'

"But the Prophet changed with the times, and there are now in
Utah very good schools, both Mormon and Gentile."

Mrs. Stenhouse admits that as a body the Mormons
are 'examples of industry and diligence, for to them
labour is one of the cardinal virtues.' She strongly
defends the moral character of the Mormon women, of
whom she says :—

"It is difficult for one not in the Mormon Church to understand
how the women submit to such treatment, and in consequence they
are regarded by some as spiritless, debased specimens of humanity;
but, as an authority on Mormonism has said, 'Whoever has read
debasement in the women of Utah has done them an injustice.
Some there be who are devoid of refined sentiment and the nobler
instincts of their sex, but no woman in history ever deserved more
respect and sympathy than the true women among the Mormons.'
They are taught to believe that their religion is a Divine institution,
which is to regenerate the world and restore the golden age, and that
by their submitting to the decrees of the church they help to bring
about this long hoped for restoration. If they endure heartrending
sorrow in the performance of their religion, they yet yield to the
Mormon doctrine that 'the first duty of a woman is submission;
the second, silence.' The men also are taught that he is noblest
who values the companionship of the soul the least, and that his

wife is but the mother of his children. Thus the poor Mormon women are often placed on the level of the most inferior animals. One of the most noted of the Mormon Apostles said : ' We think no more of taking a woman than we do of buying another cow.'

"It is never expected, nor would it be tolerated in any Mormon woman, that she should exercise her own judgment in opposition to her husband, no matter how much she might feel that he was in the wrong. I have frequently seen intelligent women subjected to the grossest tyranny on the part of ignorant and fanatical husbands who were influenced by the absurd teachings of the Tabernacle. One of the greatest Mormon writers, Orson Pratt, has said: ' The wife should never follow her own judgment in preference to that of her husband ; for if her husband desires to do right but errs in judgment, Heaven will bless her in endeavouring to carry out his counsels; for God has placed him at the head, aud though he may err in judgment, yet the wife will not be justified in disregarding his instructions and counsels ; far greater is the sin of rebellion, than the errors which arise from want of judgment ; therefore she would be condemned for suffering her will to rise against his. Be obedient, and Heaven will cause all things to work for good.' "

PASSIONS UNDER RESTRAINT.

Mrs. Whitney in her book " Why we Practice Plural Marriage " vindicates the claim of herself and her sisters in Mormondom, to be considered pure-minded women ; and she admits that it was only by strong faith and continued self-subjugation that they were enabled to overcome their natural jealousy of other women, and their desire to monopolise their husband's time and attention. As she is one of the foremost of the Mormon ladies I append an extract from her work :—

" If I did not know that my husband was actuated by the purest of motives and by religious principle I could not have fortified myself against that ' demon jealousy ; ' and had it not been for a powerful testimony from the Lord, which gave me a knowledge for myself that this principle is of celestial birth.

" I have no cause to doubt my husband's love for me

and my children, and he is a very devoted father to all his children. I know by my own experience, and that of my sainted mother's, and also of other first wives, who have acted their part nobly, that they have not only retained the affection of their husbands, but to see such a great sacrifice made by the wife of his bosom has increased his love and exalted her in his eyes. I have had this testimony from different husbands and wives.

" I assure you there is as much delicacy, modesty and refinement among those who live in this plural order as can be found anywhere,

" Polygamy is not the worst trial in the world, for it has been made honourable among our people, and it is not in the power of man nor of Congress to make it otherwise. I have always felt that I could bear it far better than those practices which are unlawful and wicked in the sight of God. That which would make me feel humiliated and disgraced before my friends and the public, would be harder to endure."

Mr. Jarman, an ex-Mormon priest, has been giving lectures in England on his experiences in Utah. The following is a brief outline of one of Jarman's lectures :—

LATTER DAY VILLAINS.

"Mr. W. Jarman, an ex-Mormon priest, stated that his grave was dug in Salt Lake City, but that he was rescued by the late General Garfield. In his lectures he occupied some time in referring to the customs and barbarous dealings of the Mormons, and declared that he was prepared to prove his assertions in any court of law. He said there were at the present day three hundred Mormon missionaries in England inducing innocent English girls to go to Salt Lake City as their wives, while they already had a number of wives in that country. He denounced the Mormons as the latter day villains, and related his escape from the Utah territory after swearing, with a dagger at his throat, that he would not divulge their secrets."

TWO THOUSAND CONVERTS YEARLY.

In conjunction with this, some editorial comments on the lectures which appeared in the papers subsequently, are interesting, instructive and apropos. The Mormons admit that their church membership is increased by the labour of their missionaries to the extent of two thousand converts per year, most of whom go to Salt Lake City. If these persons are deceived, however, I do not see why they cannot leave the city or the territory, especially, as is remarked below, the law is strictly enforced by the judges.

" It is a pity, that in his lectures on Mormonism to men only, Mr. Jarman does not adopt a higher tone in his narration. It is very painful to hear descriptions of abominable debauchery and viciousness so told as to cause repeated shouts of laughter. Many of the asserted facts might be imparted without giving minute and unpleasant details. Respecting the subject of these lectures the public should be informed that " Utah " is now *de-facto* under the United States Government. Since the formation of the Atlantic and Pacific railways a marvellous change has been made by the Federal Government in the administration of the law, as well as in the one time recognised customs of the population. The law is now administered by judges under the control of the supreme court. Polygamy is declared to be illegal, and all the wives after the first to be concubines, and their children illegitimate. Avowed polygamists render themselves liable to severe penalties, one of which is the loss of the rights of citizenship. A powerful agency in transforming the old condition of things has been the establishment there of the United States system of national education by the opening of public schools, Brigham Young, during his autocratic regime, having carefully excluded education from his system of government. The execution of Elder Lee some time since for his share in the ' Mountain Meadow Massacre ' proves how strongly the Government are making their power felt now that railway communication enables it to do so."

CHAPTER XI.

THE FUTURE OF MORMONISM.

THE last municipal elections in Salt Lake City, which caused such intense excitement—and out of which arose the revelations in open court as to the horrible oaths taken in the Endowment House—resulted in the defeat of the Mormons by a majority of about three-thousand votes. Those who are unfamiliar with the details of American life have jumped at very hasty conclusions respecting the result of this event.

An English daily had the following leader, which is typical of British ideas on the subject :—

A LIVE CORPSE.

" The days of Mormonism are numbered. Brigham Young's followers have been ousted from the dominance of Utah by the simple process of out-voting. For many years they were supreme in Salt Lake City. They founded the community; they turned a wilderness into a smiling garden, they set up their own institutions, and successfully defied the laws of the United States. All the thunders against polygamy had no effect. But the end has come in another way. The Mormons were able to evade the law, but they were not able to resist the intrusion of " the Gentiles." They could outwit the

American lawyers, but they could not stand rifle in hand on the margin of their territory, and shoot every stranger who attempted to set foot on its sacred soil. So gradually the Gentiles came in and possessed the land. The Canaanites have overwhelmed the followers of the prophet Brigham. The recent elections in Salt Lake City have left the Mormons in a hopeless minority, and all the powers of local government will pass into alien hands. This result is due in no inconsiderable measure to the one law which the Mormons have not succeeded in circumventing. Every man in Utah who is the husband of more than one wife is disqualified for the franchise. This is the most potent weapon which legal ingenuity has been able to forge against polygamy. After such a defeat the Mormons may well own themselves out-manœuvred in spite of the tenacity with which they have fought the battle for supremacy so long. In a community which is ruled by the Gentiles the disciple of Joe Smith and Brigham Young will find himself an outcast. He has lost the vote ; he is not regarded as a citizen, and he may even be stripped of the means of existence. It is quite possible that the new authorities in Utah will declare that no man living in polygamy is entitled to hold property. The enactment would probably extinguish Mormonism at a blow."

THE CHURCH IS GROWING.

This is nothing short of ridiculous to anyone who has made a study of Mormonism, or is at all familiar with American politics. The mere fact that the Mormons or "The People's Party" were outnumbered, only proves that at that particular time there were more Gentile than Mormon voters permitted to vote. Some of the Saints were undoubtedly disqualified because of Judge Anderson's decision in reference to the Endowment House oaths. Others suffered because of their having at one time practised polygamy. It is also charged that Gentile non-voters were brought into the City, and that many Mormons were illegally prevented from voting.

But even supposing that the election was fair, it in no way proves that Mormonism is doomed. The Latter Day Saints are increasing in number, although, perhaps, not in proportion to the flow of immigration to Salt Lake City of late years. Other towns are being peopled by the offspring of members of the Church, and the mere loss of local elections in itself means but little. Mormons will not hold office in Salt Lake City, but the law will not decide that a Mormon cannot hold property. The conflict between the law and the Mormons has not been of an ordinary character, and the fact that much of the violation of the statutes has been due to mistaken, but conscientious, obedience to the decrees of the Church, will always be remembered. Saints who break the law may be fined and imprisoned, but the judicial authorities will not go further and confiscate their property.

As long as the religious faith remains embedded in the hearts of the Mormons, so long will the people propagate their doctrines and endeavour to put them into practice.

IT MAY DIE OUT.

Oppression will not exterminate Mormonism. The Church may decline and fall from inherent weakness, but it will never be killed.

It may die from either of two causes.

The first is the conviction that Joseph Smith and Brigham Young were not inspired, and their revelations ought not to be obeyed.

The second is that the priesthood may lose its grip on the people. Brigham, for instance, was a far-seeing man; a clever general, whose tactics usually succeeded. Had he been alive I question if he would have allowed the local government of Salt Lake City to pass into alien hands. He would have concentrated his followers around him, so that their votes would have outnumbered those of the Gentiles. President Woodruff, the present head of the Church, is an old man, and probably failed to foresee that the Philistines were flooding the land.

HOPE IN EDUCATION.

The effect of continual contact with the Gentiles, and the consequent interchange of ideas, in all probability will have its effect on the minds of the growing generation; but it is always dangerous to adopt harsh political measures towards a whole community, and thereby give some of its more zealous members an opportunity of becoming martyrs for the sake of convincing outsiders that their cause is just. Education and firm, but fair, government will produce a more desirable effect.

During these recent elections, F. S. Richards, Chairman of the People's Party, and one of the leading Mormons, was interviewed, and asked—

WILL IT AFFECT THEM?

"' What will be the effect upon the admission of the territory into the Union by either the defeat or victory of the Peoples' Party at this election?'"

" ' It should have no effect, for the territory is entitled to statehood regardless of local politics. Doubtless the Peoples' Party defeat will tend to remove Liberal opposition of statehood, for the Liberal party is anxious for statehood soon, but not until it shall gain absolute political domination in Utah. But this act should not influence the Federal Government, for it is monstrous to make the sovereignty of a Commonwealth, the plaything of a local faction.'

" ' Will the election of the People's ticket retard the progress of the territory and immigration ? '

" ' No : Salt Lake is now one of the most safely progressive cities of America, and that progress would be continued and encouraged. Immigration of desirable citizens, all classes of investment of capital, would continue as in the past, only fictitious progress, and the influx of dissolute or idle elements are not desired.'

" ' Do your party favour admission into the Union ? '

" ' Yes, if admission can be had upon a basis of equal rights in all citizens, whose conduct is in accordance with the law.'

THE REPRESSIVE MEASURES.

" ' What is the general feeling in regard to the Edmunds and the Edmunds-Tucker Acts ? '

" ' The Liberals, of course, are gratified, as these Acts were calculated to afford them considerable and unusual help, but the people regard some features of them to the least degree unnecessary, even as to the execution of the Government's plan against the former practice of plural marriage. For instance, arbitrary confiscation of church edifices and other property is unworthy of a free government, and also giving all jury selections even in every case to the Liberals, is deemed cruelty and un-American.'

" ' What will be the result to the Mormon Church and your party in case the Gentiles win ? '

" ' I see no special result to the Mormon Church any more than to any other church. Possibly discrimination against individual members of the church might ensue. The result to our party would be the same as to any other strong party under such circumstances. Political defeat is not always permanent. It might possibly happen that all classes of citizens would help our party back to power.'

WHISKEY, WOMEN AND GAMBLING.

" ' A year ago the Liberals carried Ogden, and soon there reigned such a saturnalia of whiskey, women and gambling, that United States officials were obliged to interfere and enforce police regulations. The moral Liberals of Ogden expressed disgust with their own party, and wished the people once more in control.'

"'Are not the Mormon Church and People's Party one?'

"'Certainly they are not. The idea that they are is circulated for political purposes in order that an enactment against the Church may be used against the party. Membership or affiliation with the Church is not necessary for the People's Party standing or candidacy.'

"'Are the Edmunds' and Edmunds and Tucker Acts used for political purposes?'

"'Yes, and that was the cause of the demand by the Liberal party. Anywhere else the political minority is compelled to wait until they can reverse public sentiment, or gain a majority by legislation and accretions of new citizens; but the Liberals were too impatient for such ordinary methods, and wanted measures which would give them immediate control, and because of the unpopularity of the name of Mormon they have obtained acts disfranchising a large number of citizens, and all the women are now striving under the same cover to get Congressional legislation to take suffrage from every man who is not a member of the Liberal party.'

GENTILE FRAUDS.

"'What of the rumours of alleged Liberal frauds?'

"'Fraud and usurpation have been rampant in the legislature, and the election machinery is in the hands of the Liberals. Special registration cars were run on the Colorado line, and gangs of labourers who never saw Salt Lake, were supplied with whiskey and registered. Scores of the People's Party were struck off the lists, and in defiance of the ruling of the Supreme Court of the United States; others who have lived here thirty years were challenged on the ground of non-residence; others who were past forty on the grounds of being under the age of registration, four of whom are candidates on the Liberal ticket. The laws are declared to be supreme, and we are told that we have no redress. Inspector John Bonfield, of Chicago, is here and has exposed their frauds.'"

Governor Arthur L. Thomas, the most prominent leader of the Liberal party, a resident of Utah for eleven years, and probably the best posted man on territorial affairs, was interviewed as follows:—

"'Governor, there are rumours that the election to-morrow may precipitate a riot and serious trouble may ensue. What is your opinion?'"

"'I am of the opinion that the election will be peaceful. Both parties are working to this end.'

THE GOVERNOR'S VIEWS.

" ' How will the result of the election affect statehood ? '

" ' The Gentiles will probably carry the city by 1,000 majority. This place is the most important city in the territory and in Mormon hands. This can have no immediate effect on statehood. It will be some time, probably years, before the Gentiles will control the territory, and Utah should not be admitted as a State until a large majority of her people are in sympathy with the efforts of the Government to extirpate polygamy.'

" ' Will Gentile success affect the prosperity of Salt Lake City ? '

" ' Gentile success will mean a large increase in immigration to the city, and consequently an increase in its business and general prospects. During the past two years the increase in the Gentile population has added millions to the value of property. In fact the increase in value for the past two years has been greater than in any previous period in the history of the territory. This is directly due to the Gentile efforts. The Gentiles comprise about two thirds of the business men of the city, and own over sixty per cent. of the assessed value of the property.'

" · What has been prominent in this municipal campaign ? '

CITY NEGLECTED AND LAWS VIOLATED.

" ' There have been many local issues which have become prominent questions; the need of public improvements, of police, and in short the need of the many benefits which a Municipal Government ought to confer. After forty years of Mormon control there is not one paved street in the city ; there are no sidewalks except those laid by private enterprise; the water supply is limited, though water in abundance can be had if a proper effort is made ; a policeman is never seen two squares from Main street ; and all this is in a city of 50,000 inhabitants. In a larger sense the great overshadowing question which dominates in elections, municipal or general, is a vital issue in the campaign, this attitude of the majority of the people toward the Government under which they live. The Gentiles demand that what laws are passed should be applied, and when the Courts of last resort have decided that the laws shall be valid, there should no longer be any controversy respecting them. The law of 1862 making polygamy unlawful was flagrantly violated. The same law prohibited any church corporation holding more than fifty thousand dollars worth of property. This was defiantly disregarded, and the Mormon church became a business concern in competition with its own people.' "

WHAT WILL HAPPEN?

It is extremely difficult to prognosticate as to the future of Mormonism. Like many another faith it has gathered around it many adherents; and in spite of the amount of self-sacrifice it called for (on the part of women, at least), when polygamy was openly practised, converts poured into the Church and earnestly sought to win over unbelievers.

This goes to show, at any rate, that no religious creed can claim that the number of its believers and martyrs is any criterion of its divine origin. More solid arguments must be given than this, because it is evident that every time religious faith or superstitious credulity fastens upon the human mind it leads to a corresponding transformation of the life; and it is at times hard to draw the lines of demarcation between the heathen fanatic and the positive evangelical religionist.

MUST ANALYSE IT.

We must test Mormonism in a more rational and logical manner, and see if it is in accord with the highest and best in the Universe. If it is not, we should endeavour to supplant it by a higher ideal, and make the future brighter than the past.

But we must not forget to cast the silken robe of Charity around those who may have built their house on the treacherous sands, believing the foundation to be a solid rock.

Bagehot's Theory of the Evolution of Society, in "Physics and Politics," embodies the idea that Discussion was the greater motor-power which induced Progress after primitive Society had become stagnant through the repressiveness of a 'cake' of custom. This is pre-eminently an age of discussion, and unless Mormonism can submit to the closest scrutiny, as knowledge becomes more diffused, it will, like many another institution, glide into the realms of oblivion.

CHAPTER XII.

" Beware of false prophets, which come to you in sheep's clothing, but inwardly they are ravening wolves.

" Many will say to Me in that day, Lord, Lord, have we not prophesied in Thy name, and in Thy name have cast out devils? and in Thy name done many wonderful works?

" And then will I profess unto them, I never knew you: depart from me ye that work iniquity."—St. Matthew vii., 15, 22, 23.

CHATS WITH THE DEAD.

IN San Francisco there are scores of professional spiritualists. The bulk of them advertise in the daily papers just as tradesmen or theatrical companies do in England. They charge so much per revelation to the credulous believer who wants to know how things are progressing in the other world. It is a most lucrative occupation, and some of the spiritualists hold public séances, at which they predict various impending calamities which will befall the city, and hold conversations with deceased persons, who obligingly send messages to their friends on earth.

Sometimes 'Annie' is the one to whom the message is sent, and in all probability there will be about sixteen Annies in different parts of the hall. One of these is almost sure to have a dead brother, a long-lost sister, or some other relative answering to the description of the spiritualist. If so, a great impression is made upon the audience. If not, the medium tries some other name, until he finds someone who will admit that he is holding communion with a beloved relative.

This kind of thing makes me sceptical as to the genuineness of the communication between mortals and immortals. I believe that if the veil over the invisible world can be drawn aside, it will be by the pure in heart, and not by those who make their living off the transactions.

In company with another newspaper reporter I called one evening at the residence of a noted San Francisco trance-medium, and was shown into a dimly-lighted, but handsome room. We were joined presently by three other seekers after truth. One was a tall, fine-looking man of striking physique, well-advanced in years, and with the eyes of a dreamer. The other two were ordinary looking young men, except that one was dressed in mourning and seemed nervous, as if a strong-minded person could have great influence over him.

OUR PRIVATE SEANCE.

The door opened, and the lady medium entered. Mrs. Eggert-Aitkin was fair, fat and forty. She was clad in a light blue robe, and was as little ethereal in appearance as a flitch of bacon. However, her tongue was well lubricated, and she had her business at her finger's ends. As she had been a spiritualist for twenty years this was not remarkable.

She was afraid we should be disappointed, but she would see if the 'conditions' were favourable. She lowered the lights until we were almost in darkness. We formed a semi-circle around her and joined hands. Mrs. Aitken then worked up the trance part of the

business. Her body began to tremble, her head shook ;
she either feigned nervous excitement or else was really
'moved by the spirits.' At last after some little
struggling she began to talk in a high key and somewhat
incoherently.

" Hush ! " whispered the old gentleman in the corner,
" She is controlled."

I suppose he had been there before, and knew the
symptoms.

" Take hold of one of her hands," he continued,
" and see if she has a message for you."

I did so ; but she said nothing.

My friend tried to work the oracle with like result.

THE VEIL DRAWN ASIDE.

Then one of the other young men clutched her hand,
and she began to tell him a lot of things. Her remarks
ran something like this :

" I see a man, who has grey hair. His name is John.
Do you know him ? He knows you. He says he was
a friend of yours on earth. Do you recognise him ? "

The young man says, " Yes." It would have been
more curious if he could not remember some friend called
John.

" He tells me," continued the medium, " that you
have had trouble of late, and that you are in ill-health.
He says, ' Cheer up, and all will come well in time.'
He is happy in the other world, and says he will help
you all he can."

The nervous young man was greatly impressed by
this, and I again tried if the spirits had any message for
me. This time the connection was established, but

the spiritualist made several very bad guesses as to my health, my relatives, expectations, etc. One or two remarks, of course, were fairly apropos, but it would have been more wonderful if once in a while any shrewd woman's guesses did not hit the mark. The doctrine of probabilities was in her favour in this respect, and when she made a wrong suggestion she adroitly branched off on something else, or murmured some unintelligible words.

GAMBLING IN HEAVEN.

At last the grey-haired man secured her hand, and she cried:

" Ah ! Chief, how are you ? "—still in that C sharp key.

" Well, thank you," he replied. " How are you ? "

" Happy enough," said she, " it is all right up here. Troubles are all over. Persevere and you will learn more yet. I see Jim Carson is up here."

" Jim is there, is he ? " asked the dreamy-eyed man, in a solicitous tone.

" Yes ; you knew Jim, didn't you ? "

" Oh ! yes, we were great friends. What is he doing up there ? "

" He's just gone around the corner, hunting up a poker game ! "

This reply staggered me, but the old man only murmured meditatively.

" Ah ! yes, gambling was always Jim's great failing."

BEWARE OF FRAUDS.

More followed to the same effect, but the foregoing, as

an unvarnished narrative of cold fact, is a sufficient illustration of the extraordinary quackery of these professional prophets and trance mediums. Each visitor on leaving was expected to pay the woman half-a-dollar, and those of us who had not " sat " before were solicited to come around and see her privately as she would have something important to reveal to us !

Some people may be incredulous that such transparent humbug should deceive persons who in other matters exhibit an average amount of intelligence. But the fact that these mediums exist in such numbers and advertise so extensively proves that " all the fools are not dead yet," and that superstition has a powerful hold even on civilized people.

I do not say that there are no conscientious mediums. Animal magnetism, telepathy, mesmerism and many other curious forces have yet to be explained, and the imagination and credulity of the spiritualists may magnify these into supernatural communications. But to say that the awful and mysterious in nature is going to be revealed to a mercenary charlatan who retails her visions at half-a-dollar a head, is to me the height of the ridiculous, if not of the blasphemous.

IS SAUL AMONG THE PROPHETS ?

The fact that so many frauds exist should make us extremely cautious as to assenting to the doctrines or divine authority of any new prophet. Mahomet, Swedenborg, and others, have professed to have been inspired, and we should regard the claims of Joseph Smith as critically as those of any other man who has ever sought to draw people unto him and be their king. The Mormons revere Smith, and accredit him with being a most saintly man. Mrs. Zina Young, who knew him, gives this version of his character; but others testify to an entirely different state of facts. It is important that the evidence on both sides should be weighed dispassionately. We should endeavour to discover his motives in establishing the Mormon church "from all the facts and circumstances surrounding the case" as the judges say in their charge to the jury. If he wilfully practised deception, the more widely the facts are circulated the less converts will be made to the religion.

In striking contrast with the character of Joseph Smith, as delineated by Mrs. Zina Young, is the sketch of his history and account of the divine origin of the gold plates, given in Mrs. Stenhouse's work. She says:—"The founder, Joseph Smith, was a man of obscure origin, and if we may believe the testimony of his 'Gentile' neighbours, of a most disreputable character. According to the statement of his friends, about the year 1820 or 1821 he came under the influence of some revival meetings, conducted by the Presbyterians, Baptists, and Wesleyans, under which he was greatly exercised in mind, but could not determine which sect to join. In his bewilderment he gave himself up to prayer that the truth might be revealed to him, when one day while so engaged, he states he saw a very bright and glorious light in the heavens, which descended to the earth and enveloped him in its midst, when he saw two glorious personages, who exactly resembled each other in their features and likeness. After informing him that his sins were forgiven, they told him that none of the sects were the true Church of God, and he was not to go after them, but that in due time the fulness of the Gospel should be revealed unto him.

"On September 21st, 1823, he alleged that he had a second vision, in which the house seemed to be filled with fire, enwrapping a glorious personage, who declared himself to be an angel of God, and who stated that God's covenant with His ancient people Israel was about to be fulfilled; that the preparatory work for the second coming of the Messiah was about to commence; and that he (Smith) was to be the instrument in the hand of God to bring about some of His marvellous purposes in this glorious dispensation. He was further informed that the North American Indians were a remnant of Israel, who upon their first arrival in America, possessed a knowledge of the true God, enjoyed His favour, and had continued revelations until they wandered from Him, when they were brought down and many of them destroyed; but the records of the revelations had been preserved and were now hidden, and if faithful he would be the instrument who should bring them before the world. During that night and the following morning he had several other visions, in which he was instructed to go to the place where they were hidden and view them. He repaired to the Hill Cummorah, near Palmyra, New York, where he found the treasures in a stone chest, but was prohibited by the angel, (who, according to his statement, again appeared,) from touching them, being informed that they were only to be obtained by prayer and faithfulness in obeying the Lord. Four years later, on September 22nd, 1827, the angel delivered the records into his hands."

The records were said to be engraved on gold plates,

from seven to eight inches in width and length, being not quite as thick as common tin. With them was found an instrument, consisting of two clear crystals set in the two rims of a bow like a pair of spectacles, called the Urim and Thummin, which had the wonderful property of enabling the wearer to translate the plates, to see any distance, and to obtain revelations upon every kind of subject he desired.

According to Orson Pratt, " The plates were filled on both sides with engravings in Egyptian characters, and bound together in a volume as the leaves of a book, and fastened at one edge with three rings running through the whole. The volume was something near six inches in thickness, a part of which was sealed." A *facsimile* of three lines was published several years before Smith's death in "The Prophet," a Mormon journal, but instead of the characters being Egyptian, they were the pure invention of some ignorant person, and bear no resemblance to any ancient writings whatever. It is one of those self-evident frauds by which an ignorant impostor is almost sure to expose himself sooner or later.

When Smith lyingly affirmed that these records had been placed in his hands by the angel, several attempts were made to rob him of them, which, although unsuccessful, caused him so much trouble that he left his home and settled in Pennsylvania. From December, 1827, to February, 1828, he translated several of the plates by means of the so-called Urim and Thummin, which, with a copy of the characters, he sent by his friend, Martin Harris, to Professor Anthon, of New York, a celebrated classical scholar and Egyptologist. Harris states that the Professor pronounced the characters to be Egyptian,

Chaldaic, Assyrian, and Arabic, and that he entirely approved of his translation. The Professor, however, in a letter dated January 17th, 1834, distinctly denies having seen a translation of any kind, and asserts that the characters which Harris showed him were anything but Egyptian. Mr. Anthon says in this letter that the copy exhibited by Harris contained characters arranged in columns, imitating Greek and Hebrew letters, crosses, flourishes, Roman letters inverted; and that these columns were terminated by a clumsily-drawn circle, divided into several compartments decked with various strange marks, evidently copied from the Mexican calendar given by Humboldt, but so copied as to conceal the source from which it was taken.

" Harris, upon his return, commenced his functions as secretary to Smith, and while separated from him by a curtain, so as not to see the plates, he copied out what the translator read by means of the Urim and Thummin. When he had thus written out 116 pages, he obtained permission to take away his copy to read to his wife and some other persons pointed out by special revelation, but by the connivance of his wife he was robbed of it, and this portion of the manuscript was for ever lost to the Mormon prophet.

" It would naturally occur to anyone that with his constant visits from the angels, and with the supernatural powers of the Urim and Thummin, there would have been no difficulty in getting another translation of the lost manuscript, especially as the original plates were still in his possession ; but no, he received a special revelation warning him to avoid the attacks of the wicked, who would not fail to compare the new trans-

I

lation with that which had been stolen, and to signal out any discrepancies between them ; to prevent which he was to abstain from re-translating the stolen part. A neat way this to escape the detection of an imposture, but scarcely a way out of a difficulty that we should expect from a heavenly messenger.

" The translation was continued ; and during its progress the plates were by special revelation shown first to three witnesses in a vision ; and afterwards the identical plates were shown by Smith to eight others, and were by them handled and examined. The translation was completed in March, 1830, upon which a revelation was made to Joseph Smith commanding Martin Harris, under pain of damnation, to sell his effects to cover the expenses of its publication.

" Such in brief is a history of the Book of Mormon, and indeed of the origin of Mormonism. It is easy to see that having begun this religion with forged revelations, it was necessary to support it with others of a similar character. Thus Smith was always receiving alleged Divine messages, and those who had accepted the first lie could not but regard the voice of such a man as the voice of God, to disobey which was a deadly sin. This gave him an authority and power that his successor, Brigham Young, was not willing to forego, but to possess which he also must have revelations. They came at his bidding, and notwithstanding the events proved many of them false, still the people were so deluded by believing the first lie, that they accepted any explanation rather than acknowledge that they had been deceived by a false prophet."

The Rev. Alfred Rowland, LL.B., in a fair sketch of

"Mormonism As It Is," in the "Leisure Hour," gives the following interesting account of the contents of the Book of Mormon, together with remarks on the authorship of the work :—

AN 'INSPIRED' ROMANCE.

Another writer says :—

"The plates were said to contain an account of the primitive history of America, from the time of the settlement in that country of a colony from the Tower of Babel, down to the beginning of the fifth century of the Christian era. These colonists, called Jaredites, were a wicked race, who finally were extinguished by mutual slaughter, like Kilkenny cats. But about 600 B.C., another band of settlers came from Jerusalem, consisting of Lehi and his wife, their four sons with their four wives, and a few others, making a party of sixteen men and women altogether. When Lehi died there was a quarrel for supremacy among his sons, of whom Nephi was divinely appointed. The descendants of those who refused to recognise him were cursed with dark skins, and condemned to be ' an idle people, full of mischief and subtlety, which did seek in the wilderness for beasts of prey.' In other words these bad Hebrews were the ancestors of the North American Indians. In the time of Nephi II.—three days after the crucifixion on Calvary, which was accompanied by an earthquake which shook the western world—the Lord Jesus appeared from Heaven among the Nephites, and many of them believed in Him. The two races, however, continued hostile until in A.D. 384 a dreadful battle was fought—a kind of Armageddon—in which the Christian

Nephites were almost annihilated. But one of their prophets, named Mormon, had shortly before written an abridgment of their prophecies, histories, etc., which Moroni, one of the few survivors of the battle, hid in the Hill Cummorah in A.D. 420, and there they lay buried until they were revealed to Joseph Smith, who was to unite them with the Bible for the benefit of the Saints in these Latter Days. The famous Book of Mormon is a translation of these records which was made by Joseph Smith, with the aid of his Urim and Thummin; he sitting behind a blanket while he dictated to Oliver Cowdery. This witness and two others declared that an angel showed them the original plates; and shortly afterwards eight other persons, three being members of Smith's family, and by no means blameless in reputation, gave similar testimony. Beyond this there is no evidence whatever that the plates ever existed; while on the other hand there is reason to believe that, with the exception of a few ungrammatical interpolations, the Book of Mormon was stolen from a MS. romance, written by a clergyman named Solomon Spalding, who died in 1816."

IMPUDENT AND CUNNING.

Peter Cartwright, the famous Methodist Episcopal travelling preacher, writing of a meeting he had once with Joseph Smith, states :—" I found him to be a very illiterate and impudent desperado in morals, but at the same time he had a vast fund of low cunning." According to Cartwright, Smith flattered him, and sought to induce him to claim the gift of tongues, prophesy, and laying on of hands, as the Mormons had done. Peter, however, roundly abused the Prophet, and claimed that the Saints were hypocritical frauds. He adds that when Joseph Smith was a candidate for the Presidency of the United States almost every infidel in the country voted for him. He would not have been assassinated had not he and his followers burnt hay stacks and plundered people before he was thrown into Carthage Gaol. Joseph told Peter that he would rule a people which would overthrow the Government of the United States, and uprear a church which would supersede every religious body in the Nation."

An article in "Tit-Bits" on "Persons who profess to be inspired," thus comments on this book of Mormon:— Next to Swedenborg should, perhaps, be ranked Joseph Smith, the founder of the Mormon sect, which has succeeded in making converts in every corner of the globe. In 1823 Smith announced that he had had a vision of an angel of God, and four years later he declared that the same angel had given him a book, written in Egyptian characters on thin gold plates, which was the composition of a prophet whom he called Mormon. It was afterwards proved that the book had been written by a clergyman named Spalding; but Smith's pretensions were still believed in by a large number of people, who gradually gathered around them a large following, with the result now known."

Following is the testimony of witnesses to the book of Mormon:—

THE TESTIMONY OF THREE WITNESSES.—Be it known unto all nations, kindreds, tongues, and people unto whom this work shall come, that we, through the grace of God the Father, and our Lord Jesus Christ, have seen the plates which contain this record, which is a record of the people of Nephi, and also of the Lamanites, their brethren, and also of the people of Jarad, who came from the tower of which had been spoken; and we also know that they have been translated by the gift and power of God, for His voice hath declared it unto us; wherefore we know of a surety that the work is true. And we also testify that we have seen the engravings which are upon the plates; and they have been shewn unto us by the power of God, and not of man. And we declare with words of soberness, that an angel of God came down from Heaven, and he brought and laid before our eyes, that we beheld and saw the plates, and the engravings thereon; and we know that it is by the grace of God the Father, and our Lord Jesus Christ, that we beheld and bear record that these things are true; and it is marvellous in our eyes, nevertheless the voice of the Lord commanded us that we should bear record of it; wherefore, to be obedient unto the commandments of God, we bear testimony of these things. And we know that if we are faithful in Christ, we shall rid our garments of the blood of all men, and be found spotless before the judgment-seat of Christ, and shall dwell with Him eternally in the heavens. And the honour be to the Father, and to the Son, and to the Holy Ghost, which is one God. Amen. Oliver Cowdery, David Whitmer, Martin Harris.

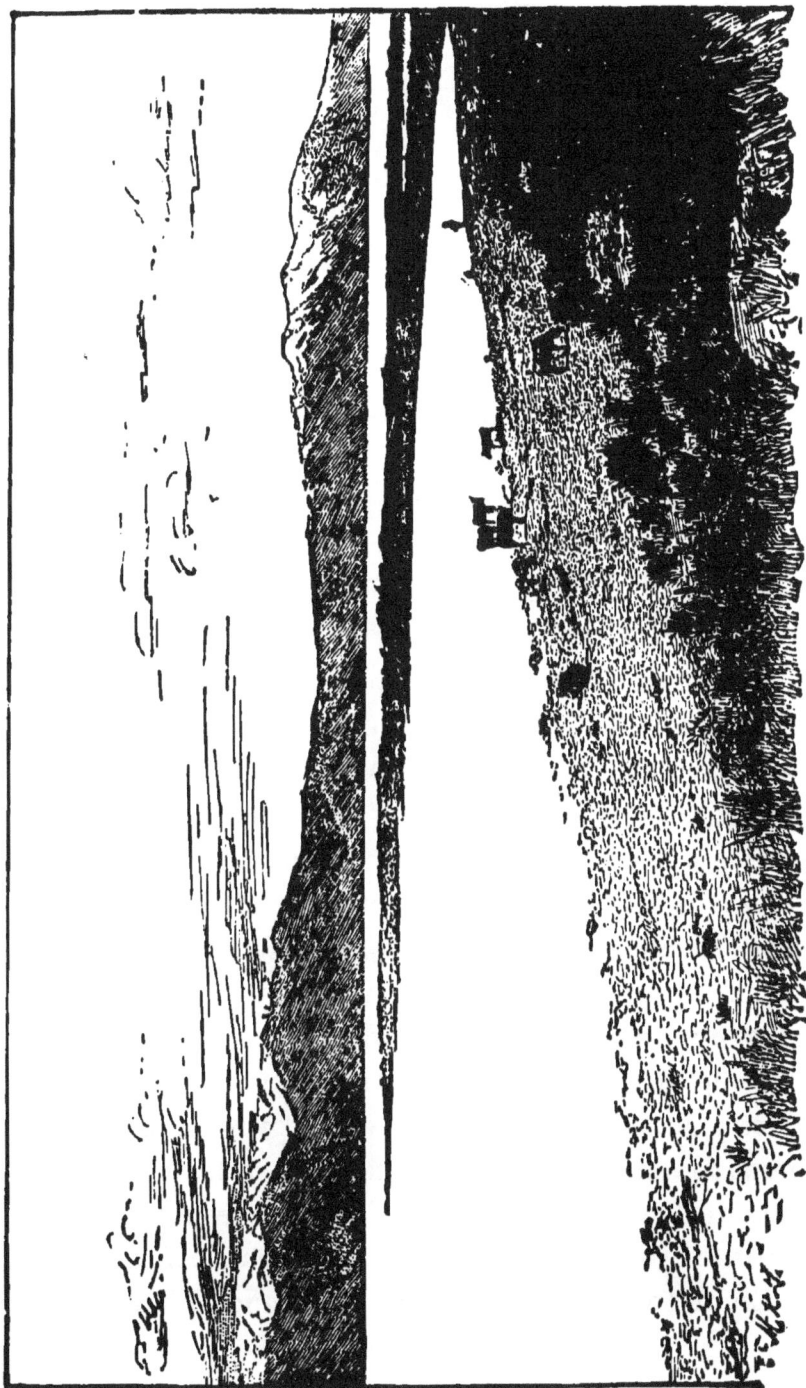

PELICAN POINT, UTAH LAKE.

CHAPTER XIII.

"And the multitude of them that believed were of one heart and of one soul; neither said any of them that ought of the things which he possessed was his own; but they had all things in common."—Acts iv. 32.

THE PRIMITIVE CHURCH.

WHATEVER vices or low ideas of morality may have crept into the Mormon religion of late years, it appears to have been one of the purest religions in early days. The editor of the San Francisco "Argonant," describing the contrast between a modern six-day's trans-continental trip in a Pullman car, with a journey made on mule back and in ox waggons through the States (which occupied five months from the time when he left New York, May 1st, 1849, until he reached San Francisco) pays this tribute to the first settlers in Salt Lake City:—"At the great city of the Salt Lake, we came upon the pioneer Mormons, camping in their covered waggons, amid corn fields just in the tassel, worshipping in a temple of boughs. Polygamy was not then acknowledged. It was a primitive church, with such primitive virtues as sobriety, industry, and honesty. There was a common field for a common granary, and communism was a feature of the primitive Christian church. Tithes were paid for the support of the priesthood—the same custom prevails in the Church of England to-day. Ignorance, bigotry, and disloyalty are charged against the Mormons—these are among the religious virtues which adorn the oldest of the hierarchical organisations. Polygamy is a crime against the law, made a crime by law, and it is in mode to denounce it, and yet it is historically venerable, by all ancient religions sanctioned."

MORMONS IN CANADA.

One American paper says that "Canada has been more thrifty than wise in dealing with Mormonism. She rather encouraged a Mormon emigration to the North-west, and it is evident that all the undesirable peculiarities of the Church which have made its existence in the United States a political and moral curse, are as fully developed in its Canadian offshoot as in Utah. One of its Canadian leaders has publicly declared that polygamy will be openly practiced, as it is now secretly a feature of life among the Mormons of our own territory."

EXTENDING THEIR TERRITORY.

Another paper has the following news-item respecting the extension of Mormon territory :—"Calgary (N.W.T.), November 18, 1889.—There is considerable excitement among the authorities at Lethbridge and Fort McLeod over the advent of a large party of Mormons from Salt Lake.City. The party includes President Woodruff, of the Mormon Church, George Q. Cannon, late Delegate in Congress from Utah, Brigham Young, Jun., and Bishop Smith, nephew of the Mormon prophet, Joseph Smith.

" Their unexpected visit is for the purpose of inspecting the workings of the Mormon colony near Fort McLeod, and to make arrangements for providing homes for several thousand Latter Day Saints, some of whom are now en route from Europe.

" President Woodruff states that, owing to the persecution of Mormons by the United States authorities in Arizona, it has been decided to make a partial change of base, and next spring thousands of Mormons now residing in Utah and Arizona will remove to the Northwest Territory. Several colonies will be established in Assinaboine and Alberta, all tributary to the one at Fort McLeod, where all the doctrines of the Mormon faith, *including polygamy*, will be taught and practised.

" The colony at Fort McLeod is under the superintendency of a former member of the British Columbia Legislature, who resigned his seat in that body to become a Mormon Bishop."

MORMONISM IN OGDEN.

On looking over an old note-book, I find an account of an interview I had with a Mormon woman in July, 1887, while passing through Utah on my way to California. My notes read as follows :—

When we reached Ogden we had to wait several hours for the next train to San Francisco, and I utilised part of the time in strolling around the town. I walked down an avenue shaded by trees with thickly clustering foliage, and sat on a bench to rest, as the weather was very hot, and the dust thick on the roads. A lady happened to be standing in her gateway, and I soon entered into conversation with her. She said she came to Ogden about five years ago. She was a Mormon, and so was her husband ; in fact his family had joined the Church before they left England. I asked her if polygamy was still practised in that town. She said, " Some of the men in Ogden have four or five wives, but are not allowed to live with them, and are constantly watched by the police, and if detected are put in the penitentiary."

" Did the Mormons live happily together before the prohibitory law was passed ? " I asked.

" Generally speaking, they did," she replied. " It is a rule for Mormons to ask the first wife if she is agreeable to their taking another, and if not they would not marry again. There are, of course, exceptions, as there would be in any community. The object of the Mormons in marrying more than one wife is that all women should have husbands, and this is necessary as there are more women than men in the world."

NOT A GOOD SAINT.

When pressed on the matter she said she did not know whether she believed in polygamy or not, and could not say what she would do if her husband desired to bring another woman into the house and the law would not prevent him. She said, " A good Mormon lady would consent, but I am afraid that I am not good at all. The Mormons believe that Joseph Smith saw an angel who inspired him to do as he did. The Mormons accept the doctrines of Christ, and found their practises on the Bible record of Solomon and his wives. I cannot understand all about it, but the Elders of the Church could argue with you, and explain things, as they are wiser than I am. The Mormons believe in a future life and that they will be rewarded, for one thing, for marrying more than one wife."

ANGELS OR BEASTS.

I said it seemed to me that either the Mormon women were angels or beasts to forgive their husband's desire to live with other women.

"They are angels," she replied, "and you will not find any in Ogden who will come under the description of beasts."

I referred to the defective civilisation of olden times, and asked her what she had to say in reply to the old argument that the Israelites were in a backward state; and that polygamy was permitted because the people were not capable of understanding and carrying out the whole of God's desires and commands.

She only replied that she thought it more honourable to have more than one wife and let the world know it, than to go with other women and deceive one's wife and the world. There were a good many Gentiles in Ogden, she said, and the Mormons had no liberty now, but they will deserve and inherit greater happiness in a future life.

COARSE VIEWS OF A WOMAN.

While travelling by train a few days ago I engaged in conversation with a gentleman who said that he had seen one of Brigham Young's widows, who went by the name of Alice, in Denver, Colorado, and was a woman of most disreputable character. "She lectured against Mormonism while there about seven years ago, and the main objection she raised against it was that women in

Salt Lake City did not have sufficient marital pleasure under a polygamous system. She was given to gross indulgence of her animal feelings, and consequently her abuse of Mormonism rather elevated the system than degraded it." The character of the witness is one of the most important elements in a criminal case, and the good must not be condemned by the testimony of the evil.

ACKNOWLEDGE THE GOOD.

A writer from Salt Lake City, named Charles Ellis, in an article on "The Iniquities of Polygamy," published in the "Detroit Free Press" a few months ago, utters some well-considered and unprejudiced remarks. He says :—"The most bitter denunciation of Mormons and polygamy to which I listened came from a woman whose face was a proclamation of the beast of passion, and she was the wife of an apostate Mormon, who was one of the most ignorant men I ever met. I found him so bitter against the Mormons that I took the trouble to trace his record, and found that he was an untruthful and unprincipled man, who was not better, but worse, than the people he denounced. In leaving the Church he sank below it. This peculiarity is true of people who leave other churches. There are two ways of getting out of a church. One is to grow out of it, the other to fall out; to go through the roof because it is not large enough to contain you, or to go out through the cellar because you have fallen through the floor. The first have nothing bad to say of their old social and religious home ; the last nothing good. When we hear denunciation of any system it is well to bear this in mind. The evils of

Mormonism cannot be cured by abusing Mormons. Let us acknowledge the good among them, and, by encouraging it, help them to outgrow the evil. That there is good one needs only to be an honest observer and a truthful reader to see. The entanglements of relationship, and that brutal proxy marriage, are things of the past. Even the Mormon people will not encourage them. They will never be repeated. God lives and grows in the minds and hearts of men and women. It will not be long before the virtues of this modern theological *mêlée* of ancient barbarisms will have outgrown the vices ; and then we shall all see that Mormonism, whatever its origin, has it place and its rights in a free country."

MORMON HYMNS.

No. 325 in the hymn book used in the Tabernacle :—

" Hail to the Prophet ascended to Heaven,
   Traitors and tyrants now fighting in vain,
Mingling with gods he can plan for his brethren,
   Death cannot conquer the hero again !
Great is his glory and endlesss his priesthood,
   Ever and ever the keys he will hold,
Faithful and true he will enter his kingdom,
   Crowned in the midst of the prophets of old."
         CHORUS—Hail to the prophet, etc.

The following hymn was composed in commemoration of the repulse of the Federal troops by " The Warriors of Zion," and was sung in the Tabernacle during a Sunday service, after the celebration of the Lord's Supper :—

" Old Sam has sent, I understand,
      Du dah ! Du dah !
A Missouri ass to rule our land,
      Du dah ! Du dah, day !

But if he comes we'll have some fun,
   Du dah ! Du dah !
To see him and his juries run,
   Du dah ! Du dah, day !

CHORUS—Then let us be on hand,
      By Brigham Young to stand,
      And if our enemies do appear,
         We'll sweep them off the land.

Old squaw-killer Harney is on the way,
   Du dah ! Du dah !
The Mormon people for to slay,
   Du dah ! Du dah, day !
Now if he comes the truth I'll tell,
   Du dah ! Du dah !
Our boys will drive him down to hell,
   Du dah ! Du dah, day ! "

Following is the chorus of one of the numerous hymns emphasising the duty of paying tithes. It is sung to the tune of " The King of the Cannibal Islands " :—

   " Then if to prosper you desire,
   And wish to keep out of the fire—
   Nay, if you to be saints aspire,
   Come forward and pay your tithing."

CHAPTER XIV.

" Phœnix—The fabulous bird which is said to exist single, and to rise again from its own ashes; hence used as an emblem of immortality."

WEBSTER.

WILL POLYGAMY BE RESURRECTED?

IS polygamy still practised by the Mormons, and will it be perpetuated?

This is an important question. We know that the doctrine of plural marriage is still tenaciously held by the Latter Day Saints, and advocated whenever the opportunity is afforded them. On the other hand, the Mormons change their base according to circumstances, and affirm, when officially interrogated, that the practice of polygamy is a thing of the past. Our Mormon guide said there had been over nine hundred convictions since the passage of the Edmunds Bill, making it a criminal offence to live with more than the first wife. This proves that the officers of the law are adopting stringent measures to make the decision of the Federal Government effective, and that it is extremely difficult for a man to violate the law and escape the penalty.

I have said elsewhere that the Mormons desire to be admitted to Statehood, so that they can make their own laws. It is to their interest, therefore (looking at it from an unscrupulous standpoint), to convince the Government that the people of Utah are law-abiding citizens; and as a matter of fact they do argue on these lines whenever the question of Utah's admission to the rights of Statehood is discussed.

THE MAIN-SPRING.

A single conversation with a conscientious Mormon lady is sufficient to convince an unprejudiced inquirer that polygamy is one of the main points of their doctrine. If this is eliminated the rest of the religion varies but little from orthodox Christianity. I do not for a moment think that the generality of Mormons believe such rubbish as that 'Adam was a God,' or in short hold any other creeds than those printed and published to the world. A few of the priests may have preached differently, but they do not constitute the whole of the Mormon Church. If then, the teaching that plural marriage is heaven ordained, be abandoned, the Mormon faith in Joseph Smith must necessarily be shaken at its foundation; and the teachers could not proselytise with any degree of success.

My opinion is that as long as the belief in the divine mission of the founder of their sect continues, so long will polygamy be a part of the Mormon religion; and this probability must be faced by the people of the United States if any legislative change is contemplated.

This is a burning matter with the dwellers in Utah Territory, and Congress has been frequently importuned to give the Mormons the same rights and privileges as are accorded to almost all other people on the American continent.

A NATIONAL ENQUIRY.

I extract a synopsis of the Report of the Congressional

Committee on Territories in regard to Utah being admitted as a State into the Union ; taken from Aunt Em's " Woman's Exponent," of March 15th, 1889 :—

" It commences by setting forth the doctrine that when Congress organises a Territory and provides a Territorial Government for the people therein, it is with the implication that they shall have a State Government, and it is with this promise held out to them that they occupy and develop the public domain ; and their right to a State Government cannot be denied, when the proper conditions are fulfilled, without bad faith on the part of Congress, unless there are circumstances that relieve Congress from a duty that would otherwise be imperative.

" The conditions in Utah are then set forth, and the statements made by the gentlemen who appeared before the Committee in behalf of Utah's admission are virtually adopted by the Committee as incontrovertible facts. The area, population, products, manufactures, mining interests, schools, churches, moral status of the people, finance of the Territory, etc., are given with details and statistics that are of great value in a public document of this character, with the deduction that the conditions exist which entitle Utah to admission as a State, and that it is of national importance that Utah should have a State Government.

" Then follow the objections, which are first, ' The existence of polygamy ; ' second, ' The power and teachings of the Mormon Church on that subject : ' Discussing these and summing the matter up, it resolves itself in this form, ' Whether a Territory will be excluded from the Union for opinions entertained by a majority of the people ; ' and also the question, ' Whether polygamy is by the Mormon Church made mandatory or permissive.' The statements on both sides are fairly presented in brief, and it is made clear that the Utah Legislature never established polygamy, and that the large majority of the people have never practised it.

" The Committee leave the dispute to the consideration of the House, with the plain reference that on a simple question of belief, Congress will not attempt to decide, and that the members of a society or sect ought to know better than their opponents what their true belief is on any article of their creed, also that this cannot well be made a basis of legislation. That Congress would hardly undertake to legislate in regard to a belief that was avowed ; certainly would not venture so far as to act against, or because of, a belief that is disputed."

WILL MAKE IT A CRIME.

The provisions of the new Constitution for Utah on

this question are thus considered, and also " the powers of Congress after admission." The document concludes with the following : —

"Notwithstanding, and in view of the fact that the present Congress is soon to expire, and probably without opportunity on the part of the House to consider this subject, your Committee deem it just to all parties concerned to present to the House the condition of Utah as to population, resources, development, schools, etc., and the extent to which polygamy exists as above set forth; together with the respective contentions as to the doctrines of the Mormon Church, and the good faith of the Mormon element in respect of the offer to make polygamy a crime by a constitutional provision, not repealable except with the consent of Congress.

"The indications are certainly very strong that in the distant future, polygamy, in fact, will have ceased to exist, and when that time arrives, if not sooner admitted, the question will have to be met, whether Congress will exclude Utah as a State because a majority of the people are members of the Mormon Church.

"Having thus presented the situation as disclosed at the hearing, the Bill is reported back, with the recommendation that it be placed on the calendar for consideration and action thereon by the House.

"From the report of this Committee one would naturally be led to the conclusion that Utah would be admitted into the Union of States in the near future. Great credit is due to the Committee from Utah who have laboured so energetically to present the claims of the Territory to the President and to the Congress of the United States, and to the Honourable Delegate whose views and opinions on this subject have been so ably set forth.

"The people should not slacken their efforts because the situation of affairs seems more propitious, but still persist in the endeavour to obtain that to which Utah is justly entitled. Perhaps after a long series of importunities it may be, like the story of the woman in Scripture, importuning the unjust judge, who granted her prayer at last because he was wearied by her persistency."

THE SWEET BY AND BY.

This is indeed a most favourable and sanguine report, but the sentiment of the American people as a whole is not so favourable to the Mormons. They assert that when once Utah is admitted to Statehood she will re-establish the practice of polygamy. This, of course, is

K 2

the reverse of what the Latter Day Saints state they are willing to promise, as is seen from the report.

How far the Mormons may be trusted in their promises is problematic, as, like the Jesuits, they appear to consider the end justifies the means. Ex-president John Taylor when doing missionary work in France denied that the Saints practised polygamy, although he had five wives at home. Mr. Rowland offers a sensible solution of the Statehood difficulty by advocating national regulation of laws respecting marriage and divorce, which now widely vary in the different States, so that Utah might don the robe of Statehood, and still be subject to regulations prohibiting polygamy.

Both the American and National Bar Associations are agreed as to the expediency of Uniformity in the Marriage and Divorce Laws. These two Federal Associations are endeavouring to bring about this most desirable Reform, as well as the International Codification of the leading principles of the laws of nations, such as arbitration, maritime rules and regulations, and criminal extradition, with a view of uniform and enforced comity among the civilised and commercial nations of the world.

Extract from the Revelation given to Joseph Smith, at Nauvoo, July 12th, 1843.

"And again, I say, let not My servant Joseph put his property out of his hands, lest an enemy come and destroy him—for Satan seeketh to destroy—for I am the Lord thy God, and he is My servant; and behold! and lo, I am with him, as I was with Abraham thy father, even unto his exaltation and glory.

"Now, as touching the law of the priesthood, there are many things pertaining thereunto. Verily, if a man be called of My Father, as was Aaron, by Mine own voice, and by the voice of Him that sent Me, and I have endowed him with the keys of the power of this priesthood, if he do any thing in My name, and according to

My law, and by My word, he will not commit sin, and I will justify
him. Let no one, therefore, set on My servant Joseph, for I will
justify him ; for he shall do the sacrifice which I require at his
hands, for his transgressions, saith the Lord your God.

"And again, as pertaining to the law of the priesthood; if any
man espouse a virgin, and desire to espouse another, and the
first give her consent ; and if he espouse the second, and they are
virgins, and have vowed to no other man, then is he justified; he
cannot commit adultery, for they are given unto him ; for he cannot
commit adultery with that that belongeth unto him, and to none
else ; and if he have ten virgins given unto him by this law, he cannot commit adultery, for they belong to him, and they are given
unto him ; therefore is he justified. But if one or either of the ten
virgins, after she is espoused, shall be with another man, she has
committed adultery, and shall be destroyed ; for they are given unto
him to multiply and replenish the earth, according to my commandment, and to fulfil the promise which was given by My Father before
the foundation of the world, and for their exaltation in the eternal
worlds, that they may bear the souls of men ; for herein is the work
of My Father continued, that he may be glorified.

" And again, verily, verily, I say unto you, if any man have a wife
who holds the keys of this power, and he teaches unto her the law
of My priesthood as pertaining to these things, then shall she believe
and administer unto him, or she shall be destroyed, saith the Lord
your God ; for I will destroy her ; for I will magnify My name upon
all those who receive and abide in My law. Therefore it shall be lawful
in me, if she receive not this law, for him to receive all things what-
soever I, the Lord his God, will give unto him, because she did not
believe and administer unto him according to My word ; and she then
becomes the transgressor, and he is exempt from the law of Sarah,
who administered unto Abraham according to the law, when I commanded Abraham to take Hagar to wife. And now, as pertaining to
this law, verily, verily, I say unto you, I will reveal more unto you
hereafter, therefore let this suffice for the present. Behold ! I am
Alpha and Omega. AMEN."

This communication on the subject of what is called
" The Patriarchal Order of Matrimony," was made
twenty-three years after the first revelation ; and nine
years more passed before this secret revelation was
publicly proclaimed. On August 29th, 1852, Brigham
Young produced in a public meeting in Salt Lake City, a
copy of this revelation, said to have been made to
Joseph Smith at Nauvoo, in which he was commanded

to take as many wives as God should give him. In justice to Emma, wife and widow of Joseph Smith, it should be stated that she denied he had any wife but herself, and declared that Brigham Young's 'new' revelation was a fraud. She withdrew to Nauvoo, where she and her four sons founded a monogamic Mormon community called Josephites. The great bulk of Mormons, however, regard the doctrine of polygamy as emanating from Joseph Smith. Even at the present day the Mormons are divided on this question. Joseph Smith, the son of the founder of the Latter Day Church, who is now fifty-eight years of age, is the leader of twenty thousand disciples in Iowa, who accept the Bible and the Book of Mormon, but repudiate Brigham Young's polygamy doctrine. A recent dispatch from Lamoui in that State says that they will maintain missions in Salt Lake City for the purpose of warning Brighamites of the crime and folly of polygamy,

MEMBERSHIP OF THE MORMON CHURCH IN SALT LAKE CITY.

The Mormon Church in Salt Lake City has 12 apostles, 70 patriarchs, 3,919 high priests, 11,805 elders, 2,069 priests, 2,292 teachers, 11,910 deacons, 81,899 families, 119,915 officers and members, and 49,303 children under eight years of age. The number of marriages for the six months ending 16th April, 1889, was 530; number of births, 2,754; new members baptised, 488; ex-communications, 113.

CHAPTER XV.

"I hear your message, but I have not faith—
And Miracle is fond Faith's favourite child."

DOGMATIST—"Well I'll maintain it—spite of sneer,
          Or argument or gibe uncivil—
       I see a thousand devils here,
          Which proves the being of a devil."

GOETHE.

IS MORMONISM OF DIVINE ORIGIN?

THE claims of any religion which is tenaciously held
by its adherents are such that we should not lightly
brush them aside. As a rule men cling to their own
religion, and regard it as a sacred thing which must not
be made the subject of critical enquiry; yet they seldom
reverence in the slightest degree the different belief
adopted by another man, or community of men. This
is manifestly unfair; since belief is an indispensable
element in all; and the diversity of religions on the face
of the earth, together with contemporaneous unbelief in
any religion at all, entitle every religious creed alike to
earnest consideration.

The same method of criticism should be adopted
towards all. Absolute certainty in spiritual matters is,
we know, unattainable—at least in our present state of
finite knowledge, in spite of the vaunting assertions of
the arrogant religious bigot. We can only deal with
the probabilities, according to our human experience and

the light of our reason, heart, and the intuitions or spiritual perceptions—the latter, however, being given no great prominence in the discussion, since they are the most controversial. We cannot expect to convince a man that the subject of our belief is an actuality because we feel it to be so. We must appeal to the enquirer's intelligence, and his own intuitive perceptions, or impressions based on the intuitions.

DOES A DIVINE BEING EXIST?

It is unnecessary to discuss at length the questions of whether or not a Divine intelligence exists? and consequently, whether any religion may, or may not, have a divine origin? But a few words will suffice to state the positions taken by persons of antagonistic modes of thought.

The intelligent believer in God, who does not confine himself entirely to spiritual feeling, usually points to, as a proof of the Creator's existence, the adaptation which is manifested in the universe—if he is asked to state his reasons—claiming that this adaptation implies design; hence there must have been a designer.

A camel before starting on a long journey across the desert can imbibe sufficient water to enable it to march many days without perishing of thirst, and its cushioned feet are adapted to the shifting sands. This would seem to indicate that the camel was specially designed by a Creator to traverse the desert in this manner.

" But," says the positivist, " there may have been a time when the desert was not a desert; when the camel was of different shape and capacity from what it is now; and when, after long ages, the sand appeared, the camel was compelled to adapt itself to its changed environment, or else die out. Such animals as could not suit themselves to the new circumstances would become extinct. Those which, by an evolutionary process, grew feet which could traverse the sand easily, and could endure long journeys before reaching an oasis, would be the camels such as we see them now. This, therefore, does not of necessity imply the existence of a conscious, intelligent designer."

The same answer is made when the believer points to the colour of the Negro, and his ability to stand the intense heat of the African climate. Sceptics say that the Negro may not have been thus originally constituted, but became so in conformity with Nature's laws as a creature of circumstances. The adaptation of varied races to different climates, and the transmutation of matter to serve a hundred uses, they say, do not warrant us in attributing these to design and a designer.

MEN NOT WORLD MAKERS.

If we argue that as a watch pre-supposes the existence of a watchmaker, and reasoning from analogy, contend that as mind was employed in making the watch, there must have been a First Great Cause, possessing infinite mind, to have launched this universe, with all its stupendous mysteries, into space, and to have kept it in order ; we are warned by scientific thinkers that we have had no experience in world-making ; and that our human experience is not a safe foundation upon which to rear a structure of positive assertion in regard to the creation of a world which transcends the loftiest flights of imagination, much less the actual facts of human life.

These persons deny the feasibility of any attempt to prove the supernatural by natural faculties. They assert that reason will not form a pathway up to a moral governor of the world, and that the intuitions must not be regarded even as facts, while as judges of what lies beyond the veil they are as flimsy as a spider's web.

THE AGNOSTIC VERDICT.

In short they say we can demonstrate nothing outside of the operation of Nature's laws ; and, therefore, that no religion can be decided to be of divine origin.

The common sense of mankind is, however, opposed to such positions, difficult as this materialistic logic may be to controvert ; and human beings, while knowing that until they pass over the dark river of death they will never absolutely be able to demonstrate the truth of their faith, still regard it as safer and more natural to cling to a belief in a God, and a God of Greatness, Justice and Mercy (rather than refrain from using the faculties with which they have been endowed), and build up, to the best of their capacity, ideas as to the Divine origin of life, heart, soul, will, conscience and matter. There may be a God ; and, as far as human experience goes, the greater probability exists that there is a God, than that the complex machinery of Nature works harmoniously because of the involuntary attraction of atoms possessing affinity. The latter theory, known as the Atomic theory, is, perhaps more intelligible, thus stated :—That Matter and Motion are eternal ; that the Ultimate Atoms which form the Universe always possessed an affinity for each other ; in the same way that there is said to be an affinity between persons of the opposite sex who are involuntarily attracted toward each other, and united by a bond of affection. These primary atoms having affinities, rushed together, formed simple organisms, and established laws, from which other subsidiary laws sprung, and so ultimately complex organisms, such as the highest in the Animal Kingdom—Man —came into existence. This theory, however, is but a feeble explanation of the Origin of Life; for how could the attraction of matter transform the dead into the living, and the mindless into the reasoning ? The Atomic hypothesis in no way accounts for the existence of mind, will, or conscience. Hence it is, as I have said, rejected by the intelligence of the average civilised man. The latter usually leaves Metaphysical, and particularly Materialistic, speculation to those for whom it has special charms, and takes his stand on the proposition that God is a Fact.

THE MYSTICAL BECOMING REAL.

The labours of the Society for the promotion of Psychical Research, by the way, in the investigation of dreams, premonitions, apparitions, mesmerism, telepathy or spiritual telegraphy, the divining rod, haunted houses, spiritualism, coincidences, etc., go to establish an even stronger supposition in favour of there being supernatural agencies at work, and that there is a connection between Human Mind and Divine Mind, which ultimately may become established truths. The realm of Realism is expanding, and the believer in God cannot be looked upon as merely a superstitious, or credulous, individual.

I assume in this study and trial of Mormonism that God exists, and that a Religion *may* have a Divine origin.

THREE GREAT TESTS.

What are the tests which should be applied to a religion, on which we may, as rational beings, form sensible conclusions as to its Divine origin?

TRUTHFUL WITNESSES IN LIEU OF PERSONAL OBSERVATION.

(1)—The most convincing test would naturally be that as to the historical facts respecting its origin, whether its alleged prophets, priests and reporters (or chroniclers) lived, spoke and wrote in the manner attributed to them —in other words, whether events and utterances have been accurately reported. In relation to alleged spiritual manifestations, such as miracles, inspiration and angel's visits, the reliability of the witnesses' testimony is of the utmost consequence. If this test results satisfactorily, no other test whatever is necessary. Whenever other tests have to be applied, it is tantamount to a confession that this test cannot be answered so as to place the matter beyond reasonable doubt.

WEIGHED IN THE BALANCE.

Another test to which a religion may be submitted is this :—Does a comparison of its doctrines with those of other religions show it to be spiritually and morally superior, and to harmonise more fully with the known facts of human nature? If so, there is a strong case of probable evidence as to its Divine origin, established. This necessitates a close comparison of the teachings of different religions, taking into consideration the varied environments of the religionists.

ITS UNIVERSALITY OF ADOPTION AND APPLICABILITY.

One of the most common arguments, and which is voiced by learned theologians, is that the thing which exists under widely different circumstances; which survives transformations in society, and prospers among different nationalities—is the True. That is to say, in regard to religion, a belief which can number its adherents by millions in many countries and ages, which accords with historical development, and forms the active principle in the lives of millions, would be the belief based on the True.

There is scarcely sufficient allowance made in this proposition for the credulity or faith of mankind, and its effects on their actions, unless the position be qualified considerably.

CREDULITY AND FAITH.

From the time that man first possessed intelligence he instinctively feared or venerated the unseen powers.

Whether man when first created was a rational and intelligent being, who descended in the scale until he became the savage who has been discovered in primitive ages; or whether the savage is the product of evolution, having been developed from the lower animals, and civilised man the result of the development of the barbarian—is one of the most disputed subjects of the day.

But a community of people, savage or civilised, has, I believe, hardly ever been discovered in which there was not some rude worship of the unknown God. The idol-worshipper's feeble mind was contented with a block of wood or stone for a deity. Some adored, and still adore, the sun, fire, ' sacred ' animals of the lower order, and men. Intelligent humanity seeks behind the effect for the Cause and worships God, the Omnipotent.

The aspiration of the human mind is for light. The grander and nobler the religion, the more likely it is to win its way among men. A religion which is in touch with the common pulse of humanity may have its persecutions and its martyrs, but ultimately will spread and be adopted by the great suffering masses of the world. The purer the ideal the more likely is its cause to permeate human society in the course of time; because it harmonises with the most delicately-attuned conscience.

It is natural, therefore, that the religion which appeals most to the intellect and the heart will be promulgated with zeal, and that the seed sown will increase a hundred-fold. This, I admit, raises a presumption in favour of the superior religion that it is a true religion ; but it does not establish the fact, nor as an isolated argument is it strong evidence of probability. There is the possibility that another religion, purer and better than any yet known, may be conceived, and until each religion, at any rate, has a fair opportunity of laying its doctrines fairly before the world, it would be unfair to judge the cause by its success or failure.

Perhaps Christianity has stood the fire of criticism, and the lapse of centuries, better than any other creed among men whose minds are above irrational superstition : but this would have to be proved before we could say that this raises a presumption in favour of the Divine origin of Christianity, and consequently that the origin of competitive religions was only human. It may not be necessary to decide on this matter before finding a verdict either for or against Mormonism.

If considerable doubt arises respecting the credibility of the witnesses, the believer may justly demand that probable evidence be entertained, and then it will be necessary to discuss the universality of its adoption or otherwise ; and its superiority or inferiority as compared with other religions. In certain cases these two tests would not be requisite ; for instance, if the historical statements were disproved, or if they were proved ; because that would finally dispose of doubt. When the supposed facts are neither disproved nor proved, but remain enshrouded in mystery, the other tests may be carefully applied, such as in the case of Christianity, for instance, where the probability exists, from *primâ facie* internal evidence—its doctrines and experiences of its believers—that it is of Divine origin.

Like the Rev. Joseph Cook of Boston, I wish to 'stick to clear ideas,' and I have made the above observations for a definite purpose. I have emphasised the conditions under which all the tests I have named would be rendered necessary ; because there are circumstances under which some of them may be considered superfluous.

If we discover on applying the test as to the truthfulness of a religion's witnesses, that there is convincing evidence of deception, fanaticism and irrationality connected with its establishment, we shall not require to go farther, as this would easily prove the religion to be of only human origin. At this point I will not say whether my conclusions as to the divine revelations to Joseph Smith will be adverse or not ; but I will say that perhaps we shall not require to consider probable evidence to any great extent, unless there is no positive destructive evidence given, and the presumption of doubt is in its favour. If one test settles the matter the reader will doubtless scarcely regret that we shall not have to go all over the histories of the multitudinous religions now extant ; or into a microscopic analysis and comparison of their doctrines.

CHAPTER XVI.

"He that believeth not shall be condemned."

JESUS CHRIST.

THE TRIAL OF MORMONISM.

THE Public Prosecutor appears for the Enquirers. A Mormon Advocate represents the Church of the Latter Day Saints. The Jury, of intelligent human beings, have heard the evidence, and the Judge turns to the Counsel for the defendant.

"Your client," he says, "is not charged with a criminal offence, in having propagated doctrines which are perhaps believed to be true and beneficial to the human race. But the Public Prosecutor demands that you shall justify the claim of your religion that it has been established by divine command in a miraculous manner. If you fail to prove this to the satisfaction of the jury they are entitled to disbelieve its divine origin. You are most zealous in proselytising, and in the interests of those persons who may only have heard one side of the matter, before this action was brought, the Court deemed it necessary that you and the people should have an opportunity of appearing here—the one, so as to speak as Exponent and Defender; the other as dispassionate Critic and Agnostic.

L

NARROWING THE INQUIRY.

" I shall instruct the jury that absolute certainty in religious matters, of which we can have only a subjective perception, is unattainable. But as rational men and women, they may perhaps entertain no reasonable doubt after hearing the evidence on both sides of the case. As Counsel for the defendant you may address yourself to the jury on the question of the origin of Mormonism. It will not be necessary to discuss in this trial whether polygamy is superior to monogamy, or *vice versa* ; or whether Mormonism is widely believed or not. The question is, are you prepared to take your stand on the ground that the book of Mormon is of divine origin ; and that on its face it bears evidence of the truth of this assertion ? If so, you may make your argument on this point. If the verdict goes against you, any practices which may have been established through your belief, must necessarily be treated as human institutions, and the public must be judges as to whether, if they fall below the standard of morality adopted by the common sense of progressive human beings, these practices should be condemned and suppressed."

THE MORMON DEFENCE.

" May it please the Court, and ladies and gentlemen of the Jury," begins the Defendant's Attorney, " I accept the suggestion of His Honour, and shall confine myself with pleasure to the testimony bearing directly on the matter of the supernatural revelations and miraculous origin of the fountain of Mormonism. This really is the point of the whole matter, as I am free to confess that if we did not esteem it a Divine command to set up our

Church and put into practice the system of plural marriage (formerly in vogue among God's chosen people, the Jews)—I say, were it not for a special revelation to that effect, we should not have departed from the monogamous standard of morality, which is approved— although violated in numberless instances—by people of modern times. Consequently we cannot, and do not, expect our system of plural marriage to prove the Divine origin of our religion, although I am far from admitting that if this system of morality were adopted by conscientious people, it would compare unfavourably with any other popular standard. I say we are willing to let plural marriage defend itself, and we stand or fall by the unbiased verdict of reasoning man on the evidences regarding the Revelation.

" I am also willing that the test of the universality of the adoption and applicability of a religion, as a probable proof of its Divine origin, should not be applied to Mormonism, because on the face of it this course would be unfair. Some religions are 2,000 years old ; Mormonism is only about sixty-seven years old. Give each religion a fair start, let it work its way along through the ages, and then this test might fairly be applied. But how can you judge different religions by their success or failure when the Latter-Day Revelation has not had time to be promulgated, and to persistently break down the barriers of superstition and error ? Mormonism is young; other religions are old : therefore that test could not have any practical bearing on us if the facts respecting our illustrious founder's visions and mission were enveloped in mystery.

L

TARES AND WHEAT.

" I appeal to you on the facts. I do not pretend to you that because we have good men and refined women among our ranks, that this is a proof of the truth of our religion. Neither do I think that because villains, treacherous scoundrels, murderers and lascivious persons have been found among us, as the tares have been found among the wheat, that this is any indication that our belief is based on falsehood. Some of the best of men have been attached to the worst of religions. Some of the worst people have been hypocritical, professed converts to the purest of religious doctrines and churches. I mention this that you may lay aside any prejudice on either side—if you may have been tempted to entertain such a prejudice.

UNITED, YET DISTINCT.

" I do not forget that we hold our Church to be an extension of the great Christian Church, and that the great majority of our members are firm believers in the doctrines taught by Christ. Whatever controversy there may be as to the divine origin of Christianity, it does not assist, or act to the detriment of, my client. We do not claim that Joseph Smith was God, or that he was the Son of God ; therefore, in judging this new dispensation we have not to prove either of these assertions. We are not required to prove that Christ performed wonderful miracles, or that the apostles saw angels, and witnessed the Resurrection and Transfiguration on the Mount. But we have to demonstrate to you that Joseph Smith saw angels ; that he, like Moses, had commandments written on tablets presented to him, and that he was not an impostor.

NOT A DIVINE PERSON.

"Christ spoke to man, we are told, as one having authority, as a divine personage, commanding people to walk in His footsteps. We set up no such right to a control over your actions. If Christ was divine, he had a right to issue supreme commands, even though they rendered null and void the power of choice, and set aside the conclusions of the mind, heart and intellect. But we do not say that Joseph Smith was in this position to dictate. We know that he was a man, and although we assert that he was inspired, we do not expect you to believe it because we say so. It is a logical proposition that inspiration must not attest history, if we have to prove our inspiration by our history. We must not reason in a circle; but satisfy you, as rational beings, on fair authentic evidence. I ask you to leave your minds open to receive truth, and that you will use the faculties which our Maker has given to every non-idiotic person to judge for yourselves if we are fools or rogues.

MIRACLES MUST BE PROVED.

"I wish above all things to be candid, and not mislead your minds one step by imposing upon your credulity.

"Now as to the supernatural character of the Mormon revelation and the marvellous manifestation in connection with the discovery of the gold plates. We cannot demand your faith without advancing proofs to convince a rational person. Either we must establish the truth of our religion by a preponderance of evidence, and satisfy your minds beyond all reasonable doubt, or I am sure you would say, and justly so, ' Joseph Smith was an impostor, and his revelation a fraud.'

" I take it that you all are agreed as to the existence of God; because if you do not assent to this rational assumption, you must of necessity disbelieve in the claims of each and every system of revealed religion. I consider that you admit the possibility of miracles, inspiration and angel visits; only, as you may never have experienced anything of the kind, you desire satisfactory evidence that the possibility is a reality.

WHAT ARE THE FACTS ?

" I come now to the testimony of the witnesses.

" We have before us the testimony of Joseph Smith,— himself a martyr to the cause he advocated. We have the evidence of three witnesses, who positively affirm that they saw an angel bring the plates and lay them before their eyes. We have the testimony of eight other witnesses that they were shown these supernatural tablets engraved with Egyptian characters. We have testimony that a professor of languages admitted some of these hieroglyphics to be what was claimed; and we have the book of Mormon itself, as a result of Joseph Smith's interpretation, containing commands to him to establish this church of Christ.

TRUTHFUL OR UNTRUTHFUL MEN.

" Remember this, there are only two issues before you. One is that Joseph Smith and the witnesses who supported him were frauds and liars, the other is that they were conscientious, truthful, and good men. You cannot set aside the testimony, or give a verdict to the effect

that these men were really religiously insane believers.
If only one man professes to see an angel he may
have been deceived; for anyone who is acquainted
with lunatics knows that the most prevalent delusion
among people possessing deranged intellects is that of
hearing supernatural voices in the night, and seeing
visions which exist only in the disordered imagination.
I have many a time seen lunacy commissioners apply
this test to people brought before them for examination.
If the subject confesses that he is troubled with supernatural demonstrations, these cold-blooded men forth-
with consider the case fit for therapeutic treatment; for
they do not believe that if the mind and body are in a
healthy and normal state, anyone would be troubled with
these visionary terrors.

" But here we have several witnesses who swear that
they also saw the angel lay the plates before their eyes;
while eight others state that the plates existed, and
were so tangible that they were given a view of them.
It is not likely that all these persons would have been
deceived at the same time and on the same state of
facts. Two madmen seldom have precisely the same
delusion, and it is highly improbable that if these men
were together they would all have been deluded in like
manner.

" As intelligent persons, therefore, you cannot adopt,
what you might deem an easy and charitable course, and
say 'They were religious lunatics; deluded zealots;
imaginative fanatics.'

THE KERNEL OF THE MATTER.

" The points you must consider are—
" ' Were these men rogues or good men ? '

" ' Did the plates exist ? '

" ' Did the angel appear ? '

" ' Was the translation of the characters genuine ? '

" Here comes in an important question, ' What motive could either Joseph Smith or his colleagues have had in propagating untruth, and setting up a religion whose institutions were in antagonism to the laws of the United States ? '

" If a man goes wrong it is a common saying— ' Who was the woman ? ' Ungallant as this may be, it implies the existence of a motor-power strong enough to overbalance the good intentions of the average man. Similarly we must look for a motive, if the truth regarding the origin of Mormonism depends on the credibility of its witnesses.

" What would they have been likely to gain from the establishment of a false religion ?

" A man who is rogue enough to seek to deceive persons by setting in motion such a tremendous and intricate piece of machinery as a bogus religious church, would surely be smart enough to consider its probable effects on his own fortunes. But what do we find ? This man Joseph Smith, who you are asked to believe was an impostor, a lascivious scoundrel reeking with immoral desires, and building up his empire on blasphemy; this man I say, was assassinated, as a natural consequence of his running counter to popular sentiment in regard to some of the real or supposed practices and teachings of himself and his followers.

EASY ROAD TO PLEASURE.

" As a rational man Joseph Smith would have known

that if he sought to build up a moral and religious system which was condemned by the people among whom he lived, he would have to suffer the penalty. He would be treated either as a criminal by the law, or else be sacrificed by the mob, which would be aroused by a startling innovation of which it did not approve.

" If Joseph Smith wanted to pluck ' the fruits and flowers of love,' is it not more sensible to suppose that he would have chosen a safer way? If a man is licentious and wishes to gratify his wild desires, could he not do so surreptitiously, and without running the risk of being murdered or thrown into gaol? I affirm that the promulgation of a religion embodying doctrines which would be dynamite under the feet of the preacher, is one of the strongest evidences that Joseph Smith was not instigated by a sordid, ambitious, or immoral motive, in announcing his mission and publishing his revelations; and that the same may be said of those witnesses who swear they also saw the angel and knew the doctrines to have been of divine origin.

" I ask you in the face of such evidence as this, are you prepared to deny the right we have set up? Are you convinced that our founder was a black-hearted villain, playing on the weaknesses and credulity of superstitious people? I ask you to reflect before you make your decision.

A REVELATION NEEDED.

" Remember that those who knew Joseph Smith intimately pronounced him to be a prayerful and noble man. If he possessed any title to this character he would not have been guilty of swearing falsely and uttering blasphemies. Remember the state of depravity and irreligion which is but cloaked in civilised countries with the garment of respectability and hypocrisy. If revelations were ever made to man, they are as badly needed in our day as in byegone ages. There is but a thin veil between this world and the mysterious world beyond. You and I are but spirits—as miraculous as anything that the mind of man can conceive. We see but the effect—the cause lies beyond. Remember that revelation is not impossible, and that men have afore-time stoned, crucified and shot, and burned those who would fain have lifted mankind to a higher plain ; and who would have imparted to sinful man the news of the glimpses they have had of supernatural glory.

" If there is a personal God and we are responsible beings, is it probable that he would have left this world in the darkness of ignorance and impenetrable mystery ? We claim that our religion is a part of the great infinite ocean of Truth. Two thousand years ago a great revealer came upon earth. Sixty-seven years ago the Latter Day revelation was made. Christ was crucified ! Joseph Smith was assassinated ! "

CHAPTER XVII.

"Thou art weighed in the balances, and art found wanting."

Daniel v. 27.

THE PROSECUTING ATTORNEY'S REPLY.

THE defender of Mormonism having closed his argument, the People's representative rises to reply.

" My task is an easy one " he says. " I do not wish to disparage the ability shown by my learned friend in laying his case before you. He has stated the issues with lucidity and candour. He has, while keeping within the limits of legal propriety, in a brief and succinct argument laid before you the evidence he has been able to accumulate on behalf of his client. We might have had a ranting appeal for eternal justice ; we might have been treated to a brilliant panegyric on the speculative good qualities of Joseph Smith ; but these would have had no effect on your minds, and my learned friend very properly refrained from appealing to your passions or sympathies, rather than to your judgment as men and women aspiring to that which is highest and best in the universe.

" I shall follow his example, and confine myself to terse, logical remarks, bearing in my heart no prejudice against the defendant ; but anxious only that truth should prevail. Rational belief is one thing, superstitious credulity is another. It will be my duty to point out to you that the Mormon religion appeals to the gullibility of impressionable people; for the evidence adduced before you has proved this beyond all reasonable doubt.

WHY THIS MYSTERY?

" We are not surprised to find that, as nearly two thousand years have elapsed since Christ lived on earth, his acts are the subject of extensive controversy, and that a much greater demand is made on our faith than was the case with contemporaneous human beings, who saw and heard him time after time. Remembering that there were no newspapers in those days; that practically Palestine was isolated from the rest of the world, and that they had no electric wires to flash news from one continent to another, or mighty vessels to carry thousands from one side of the globe to the other within a month—remembering these facts, and that the average intelligence was much lower than to-day,—I say we are scarcely surprised that the enquirer now finds the external evidence as to its central personage to be very scanty; and we naturally study the gospels, and other documentary testimony, with all the greater zest and persistency, because upon these, almost exclusively, we are asked to base our belief in its divine origin.

" But we do not expect to find the same mystery surrounding the facts in connection with the foundation of the Mormon Church. The alleged revelations only date from 1820, yet there is such a conflict of evidence as to the main features of the religion that we are tempted to exclaim—Is there any truth in history? Can any statements be made which in a few years will

not be controverted? The burden of proof, however, rests with the Mormons, as it is impossible to
disprove the assertion of a man that he saw an angel,
except by rigidly cross-examining him, and detecting
discrepancies in his story, or showing that he fails to
produce the very articles which are the foundation of
his claim.

" Strictly speaking there is only one question which I
need put to you. If I go beyond this question it will be
more for the purpose of aiding you in dealing with any
other religious doctrine to which some zealous missionary
may seek to make you a convert.

" WHERE ARE THOSE SUPERNATURAL PLATES?

" That is the question which cuts the ground from
under the Mormon Church. The disappearance of
' exhibits ' during the trial of a case is always of the
greatest importance. The non-production of evidence
by a defendant which he has openly announced will
establish his innocence, is most damaging to his cause.

" Where are those wonderful plates? I ask. My
learned friend has said nothing about their disappearance, so I presume it is left to your imagination to fancy
that the angel who revealed their whereabouts, also took
them up in a cloud after they had been translated. If
my friend could produce them in court we could submit
them to learned men who would have no difficulty in
deciphering them if they were written in Egyptian or
any other language, living or dead. If the characters
then formed the contents of the book of Mormon we
should be all ready to admit that so far the defendant

had proved his case, and most searching investigations would then be required to find whether they had been engraved by Spalding, or somebody else of human, rather than divine origin.

" We are told that Joseph Smith had his first revelation when he was fourteen years of age; that he believed the North American Indians were a remnant of Israel ; that he dwelt among them and was informed by angels that no sect on earth was the real Church of Christ, and that Smith was the privileged person who was to usher in the second coming of the Messiah by establishing the True Church ; that there was a 'Urim and Thummim ' in the stone box, by which the plates could be transcribed, and which possessed other remarkable qualities. I ask you whether this outline of the revelation does not bear a suspicious resemblance to the biblical narrative of Samuel's visions, Moses' tables of stone, the Urim and Thummim in the ark, and the claim of the Jews that they alone were the favoured people of God? If these two transparent stones possessed these marvellous properties they would be the strongest kind of evidence on behalf of the defence. Considering the vast number of antiquities which have been handed down from one generation to another, it ought to have been the easiest thing imaginable to produce these magic spectacles. That they have disappeared, and were not publicly shown at the time when the 'prophet' professed to have had them, is proof positive to any unprejudiced and non-superstitious mind that the whole thing was a transparent piece of quackery, worthy only of a bogus spiritualistic medium.

SUPERSTITION NOT DEAD.

" There is one lesson that you may draw from this
false religion—it is that there is more superstition in the
world than many imagine. We are accustomed to
boast of the intellectual grandeur of the nineteenth
century, but if it were necessary I could show you that
there are thousands of people both in England and
America who are firm believers in witchcraft, charms,
omens, unlucky days, and other superstitions. We need
not wonder, therefore, that people flock around the banners
of a false prophet. There is such a thing as emotional
insanity. The man who has a violent temper is to that
extent insane when inflamed with anger ; and it is hard
to draw the line as to where true spiritual intuition ends,
and irrational credulity begins. Is it surprising that men
will believe in the pretensions of others when history
abounds with instances of men who have entertained
the wildest ideas of themselves ?

THE PRETENDED MESSIAH.

"Take the case of James Naylor, the pretended
Messiah, who died in 1660. This enthusiastic visionary
was an admired preacher among the Quaker followers of
George Fox: As his features bore a near resemblance
to those of Christ, he believed he was Christ, and was
so acknowledged by a large number of people when he
assumed the character. He professed to heal the sick
and raise the dead, and when he entered Bristol, the
people of his sect strewed leaves and branches of the
trees in front of him, and cried, ' Hosannah, blessed is
he that cometh in the name of the Lord ! ' He was
pillored, burnt through the tongue, and branded with a

B in his forehead for blasphemy; and, after being whipped, was confined to hard labour. The discipline of the prison soon restored him to his senses, and he acknowledged having been guilty of a heinous sin. Here we have the case of a man who actually deluded himself; but, as my learned friend pointed out, we cannot take a charitable view of Joseph Smith's case and say he was a monomaniac, for the evidences of a concerted swindle are too palpable in his case. The case of Naylor is principally valuable as showing that mere faith or credulity even among civilised people is no criterion whatever of the genuineness of the claims of the archmover. No one would deprecate cynical disbelief in religious matters more than myself. But, on the other hand, we must beware lest we give way to impressions entirely unsupported by reason. What can we think of the absurd belief held by a native of Cornwall who died a few years ago, that he should live until the second coming of Christ? Or of the Shakers who believe in the possibility of an absolutely sinless life, and exemption from death on the ground that sin causes death, and, therefore, if they sin not, neither will they die?

NAILED TO THE CROSS.

"Or of the fanaticism of Matthew Loval, a shoemaker of Venice (who died in 1810), who believed he ought to imitate the sufferings of the Redeemer, so tried to crucify himself; piercing his side; nailing himself, naked and bleeding, to a cross, to be found next morning, by the inhabitants, bearing his sufferings with the stoical indifference of a doomed savage or the resignation of a Christian martyr?

" These extraordinary instances of men, otherwise sane and shrewd, show you that human nature is most bewildering, tortuous, and that we may well ask for strong proofs of the Divine origin of any doctrine, knowing how reason has been warped by superstition in the past. Not every man who professes to have his lips touched with the live coal from the altar is worthy of credence. How many false prophets foretold that the world would have come to an end years ago, from Mother Shipton to divines of the Church of England ? It is an old story this—the presumption of man :—

' Men would be angels, angels would be gods.'

" We may do worse, my friends, than lend an attentive ear to Pope—that poet whose reasoning has stood many an assault :—

" Heaven from all creatures hides the book of fate,
All but the page prescribed—their present state:
From brutes what men, from men what angels know,
Or who could suffer being here below ?
The lamb thy riot dooms to bleed to-day,
Had he thy reason could he skip and play ?
Pleased to the last he crops the flowery food,
And licks the hand just raised to shed his blood.
* * * * *
What future bliss He gives not thee to know,
But gives that hope to be thy blessing now ;
Hope springs eternal in the human breast ;
Man never is, but always to be, blest.
* * * * *
Hope humbly then, on trembling pinions soar ;
Wait the great teacher, Death, and God adore."

WHY REVEAL TO A FEW ?

" This teaching, you will perceive, is drawn from the book of Nature. The poet ignores revelation of a supernatural character. I do not ask you to do likewise, for revelation may be genuine. I only wish to impress

M

upon you that revealed religion goes far beyond the teachings of the book of Nature; and that before you cling to any special manifestation of this kind you should bring to bear upon the Medium of inspiration all the light of your understanding; and not be deluded by such blasphemous trickery as that of this charlatan, Joseph Smith, and his companions in knavery, the 'witnesses' who state they also saw the angel. There is no reason for any 'hole in the corner' revelations. God has given to us to see the transcendent glories of this world. If he desires us to have glimpses of the infinite, do you think He is going to single out half-a-dozen mortals throughout the world for this special favour? Are there only a few righteous men in Sodom and Gomorrah? Even if so, would not special ocular demonstrations of this kind be needed more by the ninety and nine lost sheep in the wilderness than by the one just man that needs no repentance?

"I know a man who is as sane as I am in most things; who was an electrician by profession before he retired to live on his private means; who has been a zealous student of ancient history, and has a remarkably valuable collection of old coins—all of which goes to prove that, as men go, he is not an ignorant charlatan desirous of imposing upon the credulity of men for personal gain. He told me with an air of serious conviction, something which no man would tell another in joke, and I believe he was perfectly sincere in the belief that he actually saw what he mentioned. He said:—

LIFE, ELECTRICITY, AND VISIONS.

"'You know I have had a great deal to do with

electricity. I have a belief that all Life is but electric
fire: when a man dies, the spark which is in him becomes
once more a part of the great ocean of electricity. I
had a theory that by experimenting with this mysterious
element, human beings could know more of the secrets
of the Universe. Several friends and myself combined
to make electrical circuits to transmit thought, and
penetrate what had before been hidden from man. We
went so far that we dared not go farther. We found
we were exploring forbidden ground, and my companions
became afraid. One night we continued our experi-
ments, and we heard a voice warning us that if we did
not stop, our blood would be upon our own heads. My
friends were stricken with terror and gave up the
dangerous work. I thought it might have been a
delusion, and made another attempt to prove the
mysteries. Then I saw light stream down from the
ceiling of my room and Christ himself stood before me.
I knew then that either I must be content with finite
knowledge or pass into the great sea of life. From that
moment I forswore all psychical investigation, for I know
it means destruction. I see how people now-a-days are
dabbling in electricity, and using up the great life-force
of the world. If they go on like they are going there
will be fearful convulsions of nature in the near future.'

" I ask you, as reasonable men, do you believe such
assertions as are contained in that statement? I should
have to consider you as being low in the scale of intel-
lectuality if you did. Yet if you do not disregard the
claims of Joseph Smith's religion you may as well assent
to the delusions of every monomaniac, and the pretentions of every blasphemous trickster.

EVIDENCE OF FRAUD.

" Now as to the character of the witnesses, according
to direct testimony. My learned friend has told you
Joseph Smith was held to be a good man by Mrs. Zina
Young, and others who knew him. I have adduced
testimony quite the reverse. The implication, too, that
Smith failed to translate the stolen portion of the Book
of Mormon the second time, because he was afraid of
the comparison which might be instituted, is another
evidence of duplicity. I am aware, too, that there is in
existence testimony to the effect that an interviewer
questioned the witness Harris and others, who admitted
that they only saw the supernatural visions with the eye
of faith ! I know that, strictly speaking, this is not
legally admissible, because I am unable to give my
authority for the statement, which was published in a
magazine many years ago ; but my friend can scarcely
object to my mentioning the fact, as most of the evidence
introduced here on both sides is documentary, as we
could not cross-examine writers of books who are either
dead or in foreign countries. I only desire to show that
as opposed to the written affirmation by these witnesses,
there is alleged to be an admittance by them that they
saw only with ' the eye of faith.'

IMITATING BIBLICAL LANGUAGE.

" If you will take a retrospective glance at the
phraseology of the revelation in regard to polygamy, you
will notice a similarity to biblical style ; yet there
is such a difference between the two that one cannot but
consider Smith's revelations a deliberate, and only

partially successful, imitation. It would be interesting to speculate upon the state of Smith's mind during the concoction of these things. If he believed in the Divine origin of the Scriptures, or the existence of a Supreme Being, he was guilty of wilful blasphemy, while at the same time preaching to others that the only true road to God was through himself. An artist once painted Solomon with one foot in heaven and the other in hell, because he did not know where Solomon had gone. I question if he would have the same difficulty in fixing the abode of one who deliberately set himself to pervert the most sacred instincts of humanity into polluted channels.

"I should consider you would have no difficulty in deciding that Smith received no supernatural plates or revelations; consequently the translations were frauds invented to deceive the public. This being so you cannot do other than return a verdict that Mormonism is not of Divine origin.

QUESTION OF MOTIVE.

"Before submitting the case to you, however, I would like to point out the fallacy involved in one phase of the argument of my friend, the Mormon Advocate, upon which he laid great stress—I refer to his question, 'What motive could either Joseph Smith or his colleagues have had in propagating untruth, and setting up a religion whose institutions were in antagonism to the laws of the United States?'

"The study of motives is an interesting one, but it does not turn in favour of the defendant in this case. It is contended that Joseph Smith could have obtained the gratification of any sensual or ambitious desires without facing the probabilities of assassination, and that if he was a shrewd rogue, as I claim, he would have chosen some easier and safer path.

" I admit the former clause, that he could have done so ; but deny that he necessarily would have taken that course.

" Some will tell you that Duty is one of the greatest motive powers or springs of human action; a greater one is the desire for Happiness. In pursuing this will o'-the-wisp, this flying phantom, this mirage of the desert, men choose various paths. Some find their happiness (or try to) in self-sacrifice ; but the great bulk of mankind seek the philosopher's stone along the roads of Ambition, Sentiment, Passion, Avarice, Thriftlessness, Destructiveness, and other highways congenial to different types of human beings. ' In men we various ruling motives find.' But supposing that a man is actuated by a selfish and evil motive, does it follow even if he is crafty and unprincipled that he will choose the easiest method of attaining his object? I say, by no means.

EXCEPTIONS TO THE RULE.

" Do not understand me to deny that the tendency of mankind in the pursuit of happiness is to follow the line of least resistance, or, in other words, to seek the most simple and convenient method of achieving the object in view. I admit this is the rule, but, like many other rules, this has its exceptions, and the exceptions are numerous.

" What is the object of the drunkard? Not to *drink beer*, but to derive the *pleasure*, or supposed pleasure, he obtains from indulgence in alcohol. His object is to secure happiness, and he chooses one way of obtaining it. I have heard of an old toper who said his idea of Paradise was a place where he could keep his mouth under the running tap of a beer barrel! I know many shrewd, crafty men who are confirmed drunkards. They shorten their lives, debauch and disgrace themselves, and become a pest to Society by their besotted habits. I want to know if, in this one respect, these men are not fools? To persons of refined tastes such indulgence would be productive of no pleasure ; and to no rational person would it return pleasure commensurate with the coincident suffering and loss. It is a wise saying, that it is foolish to purchase present pleasure at the expense of future pain. Yet we see this course pursued every day by persons of widely different environment. Chinese girls suffer torture when they are babies, and incon- venience through life, in order to be classed among ' the small-footed ladies.' English girls compress their waists with corsets; and this is one of the main causes to which the thirty thousand deaths annually of Englishwomen from consumption may be attributed, according to the report of the Registrar - General. Many criminals recently confessed when interrogated in America, that crime did not pay. If they had been honest they believed they might have got rich with half the expendi- ture of energy. Every foolish or vicious person, from the opium fiend, debauchee, and criminal, to the business man who ruins his health in the struggle to soar above his rivals and build up a fortune, pursues the worst course that could be chosen to obtain satisfying and permanent pleasure. Diogenes in his tub is far more sensible in being contented, providing the King does not come between him and the sunlight. Unless a man studies the laws of health and the effects of actions, and compares transitory whirlwinds with permanent gentle zephyrs, he is *not* choosing the most rational path to the attainment of Happiness.

A CRAFTY FOOL.

"Is there anything inconsistent then in Joseph Smith having been a crafty villain, and, at the same time, in some respects, a consummate fool? Assuredly not. For one thing he could not have foreseen that he was to be assassinated. If his mind was not gnarled and badly-balanced he might, however, have anticipated a calamitous end to his illegal venture. But it is a common thing for men to allow their passions to blind them to probable, and, in some cases, inevitable results. In homicide cases Judges charge the Jury that *malice aforethought* must be proved to constitute the crime murder in the first degree; and this malice is to be discovered from a consideration of all the facts and circumstances surrounding the case, as it is impossible to obtain an actual view of the operations of the criminal's mind. But it is a fact equally true that atrocious cases of slaying have often occurred, where there has been a complete absence of an apparently adequate motive for the killing. It is one of the most difficult things in the world to trace a given action to a given motive. The foolishness of the wise man, though a paradox, is nevertheless a reality. We have heard of the philosopher who had a large and a small hole made in the bottom of his door so that the cat and kitten could pass through. When asked as to his reason, he replied, ' Why, the great cat could not go through the little hole ; ' and was amazed when his interrogator reminded him that the little kitten could go through the large hole! ' The rogue and fool by fits is fair and wise,' says Pope. May we not say, ' The rogue by fits becomes a fool ? ' If not, why the saying, ' He was hoisted by his own petard ; ' ' He digged a pit for others, and fell into it himself ? ' Because a crafty man makes a mistake in calculation and suffers by his own folly, it does not follow that he is not cunning in his dealings in general. Joseph Smith might have conceived and put into practice the wildest kind of ideas, with a great display of crooked ingenuity, and yet have been so puffed up with vanity or ambition as to overlook possible and probable disastrous results to himself. Or, even foreseeing these results, he may have been so filled with the thirst for notoriety that inspires many individuals, as to purchase present happiness at the expense of future pain. What more destructive and irrational method of settling national disputes than that of going to war and slaying thousands of valuable lives ? Yet in spite of our vaunted civilisation, international arbitration has not yet superseded this savage method of settling quarrels.

" This somewhat extended reference to the difficulty of attaching a rational motive to an apparently irrational act, was in point of fact unnecessary in view of the other circumstances of the case. But, if in other respects the evidence had been in Joseph Smith's favour, the fact that he risked his life and fortune in promulgating his doctrines, might have been additional corroborative evidence as to his sincerity. As the facts are quite to the contrary, it is far from proved that because he took chances on a risky speculation, he was not a hypocritical, blaspheming, false prophet.

" In the face of this evidence you cannot accept Mormonism as of Divine origin. It would be contrary to reason and judgment. Every year the Mormon missionaries are circulating specious falsehoods to beguile girls into the meshes of their net. There are always feeble minds ready to be swayed by the first powerful influence. I appeal to you to condemn the Mormon faith as based on falsehood, fraud, and blasphemy; and to do your duty in rolling away the mists of superstition and ignorance—relics of barbarous ages—and to advocate the emancipation of thought, and the reign of truth and rational belief."

What is the verdict?

CHAPTER XVIII.

" This light and darkness in our chaos join'd
What still divide ? The God within the mind.
Extremes in Nature equal ends produce,
In man they join to some mysterious use ;
Tho' each by turns the other's bound invade,
As, in some well-wrought picture, light and shade,
And oft so mixed the difference is too nice
Where ends the Virtue, or begins the Vice."
                                              —POPE.

" Great men are always polygamists; no matter under what social
system they may live, even though they transgress the laws of
ordinary social life."
          THE HISTORY AND PHILOSOPHY OF MARRIAGE.

ARE THE MORMONS IMMORAL ?

HAVING disposed of the question as to the Divine
origin of Mormonism, we now have to consider
whether the Mormons are moral or immoral.

Persons of circumscribed knowledge of human nature
and the manners and customs of nations, usually fall
into the error of condemning other people strongly,
illogically, and uncharitably ; entirely forgetting that
morality is largely a matter of longitude and latitude, as
Superintendent White puts it in the interview I had
with him. An institution in vogue among the Sandwich
Islanders may be utterly opposed to our notions of
propriety or good conduct ; but those islanders may be

eminently respectable members of the community in which they reside ; and deserving enlightenment rather than scorn, condemnation, or ridicule.

There are many kinds of morality; and until it can be shown that a man or woman violates every one of them, we have no right to say that, because their practises are contrary to our ideas of right and wrong, they must necessarily be looked upon as criminals or vicious people. From what Dr. Talmage says of the Mormons one would be led to conclude that there was not a conscientious, moral, refined, and intelligent individual among the Church of the Latter Day Saints. Such caustic, denunciatory language is misleading, and, therefore, unjust, as can be easily demonstrated to an impartial mind.

THE CHILD OF NATURE.

There is such a thing as *natural morality*, or natural good conduct. It is the instinct of the savage to slay, but he knows full well that he is violating a natural law in murdering a fellow being. The mere fact that the individual has life, renders it a law of Nature that he should be allowed to retain his life, until for some act he forfeits that life through being an enemy of Society. While he remains non-destructive himself his fellow savage has no moral right to cut the thread of his existence, and the slayer becomes a murderer.

But barbaric morality may admit of the killing of human beings. A Hindoo mother throws her babe into the Ganges as a sacrifice to the gods. Being blinded by ignorance and fanatical teachings and customs, she crushes all a mother's love—because she believes she is doing a meritorious act and a religious duty. This is a wilful destruction of human life; yet who would say that the conscientious, sorrowing woman was an immoral and murderous wretch? This would be a case for enlightenment by spreading truer, holier, more natural beliefs, to be crystalised into nobler customs. But according to the light of her knowledge and the standard of morality in vogue among her people, this woman is a moral and religious member of Society.

SAVAGE MORALITY.

It is essential that we should dwell on this lower order of morality, because all higher standards of good conduct are matters of development. In Panama the natives walk about in a state of complete nudity, as also in some parts of Africa and other warm countries. These people have no idea that they are following any objectionable mode of life which might be styled immoral. They have their own code of morality, and this practice of Garden of Eden simplicity is to them natural, comfortable and perfectly respectable. White persons at first are intensely shocked on residing in these countries; but after a time this feeling wears off, and they view the custom with indifference, and imitate it as nearly as they can without violating the more sensitive code of morality which in colder countries they have been accustomed to conform to and approve. In this instance the natives neither violate natural morality nor any standard set up in their midst.

A savage may be guilty of breaking the laws of natural morality, and yet keep within the bounds of his own laws and customs. There is thus a distinction between natural morality and savage morality.

WALKED TO HER GRAVE.

I have heard of a traveller who, when among one of the Indian tribes, was invited to attend a funeral. On the day appointed a large party assembled, and in conversation with one of those present the traveller remarked that he did not see the dead person. ' It is my mother who is to be buried ' replied a young native by his side, ' but she is not dead yet ; she is walking at the head of the procession.' To the amazement of the visitor the old woman was conversing with her friends in the most cheerful manner, and on arriving at the burial place she submitted to being strangled as if it were an ordinary and perfectly legitimate procedure ! It was simply a custom of the tribe that when their members became old and useless they should be killed off. She conformed to the custom, and the executioners looked upon it as an unavoidable, although perhaps unpleasant, duty. To us such an act seems abhorrent—although we consider we are justified in ' mercifully ending the sufferings of the lower animals.' But should we look upon the stranglers in this case as murderers ? I say, certainly not.

VARYING STANDARDS OF MORALITY.

But besides natural and savage morality there is also civilised morality. Even here, however, scarcely any two systems are alike. What constitutes good conduct in one civilised country would be scouted in another. Some of the French and Spanish notions are repugnant to English people; while our ideas of propriety are, in some instances, equally distasteful and objectionable to people of other nations. I could specify instances, but were I to do so many would doubtless consider me guilty of great impropriety. However, at the risk of offending a few of the thin-skinned type, I will give an example.

Plutarch was certainly a man of superior intellect, and in his ideal Commonwealth of Lycurgus, he narrates (evidently with approval) some of the customs inaugurated by this 'half mythical or all mythical Solon of Sparta.' He says :—

" In order to take away the excessive tenderness and delicacy of the sex, the consequence of a recluse life, he accustomed the virgins occasionally to be seen naked, as well as the young men, and to dance and sing in their presence on certain festivals. . . . . . As for the virgins appearing naked, there was nothing disgraceful in it, because everything was conducted with modesty, and without one indecent word or action."

Startling and immoral as this Adam and Eve style would be to English people, it would be no more so than are our customs of allowing girls to walk abroad without escorts, or veils over their faces, to some of the Oriental nations.

" SOCIETY " MORALITY.

But even more curious than the broad national systems of morality, is that unwritten code which we may term Society morality—the laws of Mrs. Grundy, who stands ready to be shocked and scandalised if her decrees are disregarded. What anomalies we may perceive in her hotch-potch, patch-work ethics ! Pictures of the nude, when painted by eminent artists, are lauded as splendid studies of nature. Statues of undraped figures may be seen at the Crystal Palace and other public places, and the unsophisticated rural visitor is dumbfounded at the things which Society does not regard as indecent or immoral. But a dealer in photographs of nude men and women finds himself under the grip of the law; and an insufficient amount of clothing worn by a man on the street would also lead to arrest, and a visit to the police station. George Meredith speaking of a society woman remarked " She exposed as much of her person as modern Society regulations would allow her to do." Mrs. Grundy approves of low-necked ball dresses, and gossamer bathing suits, yet anything approaching such a costume on the street would evoke her righteous horror. I venture to say that oft-times the things which Society condemn are really less harmful or immoral in their tendency or nature, than the customs which Mrs. Grundy has stamped with the seal of her approval.

All this brings us to the inevitable conclusion that unless an individual violates a natural law there is great possibility of his or her being undeserving of disdain or punishment. Particular actions are no safe guide to us as to our attitude towards those who may perform those actions.

WHAT IS PERSONAL MORALITY.

What then is the main requisite of personal morality? I answer that a man must be above all things, conscientious. If he uses his conscience, his heart, and his intellect in a perfectly honest manner, he does not lose his claim to our esteem, although he may eat peas with his knife, or live with twenty wives.

Who would call George Eliot an immoral woman ? She possessed genius, despised the legal trammels employed to force love, and lived with Mr. Lewis without the aid of the marriage ceremony. Her actions we condemn as objectionable, illegal, bad in their influence, and—according to our own standard—immoral, yet we are given to understand that it was from a pure motive that this popular lady novelist departed from this custom of good conduct; and we have no right to withhold our respect from her.

If a person is conscientious, his errors of judgment, defects of perceptivity, training or acquired knowledge must be considered as such, and he must not be regarded as an enemy of Society.

THE SPHERE OF CONSCIENCE.

It is no longer held by right-thinking men that Conscience will reveal what particular line of action will eventually produce good results, or what religious belief is true. If this idea was not exploded, we should have to face the preposterous conclusion that if a man's life was contrary to any given and accepted system of morality, it would follow that he had disregarded his Conscience, and was, therefore, an immoral person.

The following lines, which I wrote some years ago, state in a terse manner the limitations of Conscience :—

RIGHT AND WRONG.

Actions or thoughts may good or evil be,
But human brains may vainly seek to grasp
The heights and depths of knowledge, so to learn
Beyond all doubt the ultimate effects.
Yet trust not all to Conscience' warning voice ;
She sways no sceptre in thy Reason's sphere ;

N

For know that Conscience only Motive heeds,
Interpreting thy heart's inmost desire.
Keep then thy longings spotless as the snow ;
Expand thy Mind and open wide her doors ;
Act on the light that downward freely streams,
Then Conscience will approve and God will smile.

ARE MORMONS CONSCIENTIOUS?

Conscience being only the interpreter of " rightness
and oughtness in motives," we must not blame conscientious Mormons because their ideas differ from ours,
both as to their religious belief and moral system. As
they do not violate the law of natural morality they are
entitled to have their actions and belief discussed as
things apart from themselves ; and every facility should
be afforded for educating them to ideas and practises
in harmony with the highest standard of morality,
which is the result of the combined experience of
civilised man, as elicited by a comparison of the nature
and effects of things.

If there were no good people among the Mormons,
there would have been little reason for a thorough
investigation and discussion of their lives. We should
simply need to dispatch missionaries to them to mould
them on the lines of civilisation, as far as practicable.
But I write to condemn the system, and to defend the
bulk of the people from the attacks often made upon
their character as a community ; for I believe, after fair
consideration of testimony and from personal observation,
that the majority of the Saints are mistaken but conscientious, and, therefore, moral people.

SHEEP AND GOATS.

That there are glaring exceptions to this class I readily

admit. Whoever was responsible for the Mountain Meadow massacre ; the institution of the law that an apostate must die; the callousness displayed in sending deluded believers to Utah under the Hand-Cart scheme, and many other things mentioned in this book—must be considered as evil-minded, selfish, murderous and immoral people. Joe Smith and Brigham Young are dead, so we are not required to place them on trial for the deeds done in the body ; but we are bound to form the opinion that while the Mormons have been at times persecuted, they have sometimes exacted an eye for an eye and a tooth for a tooth—sometimes the wrong eye and tooth. We have heard of the rack, the thumb-screw, the scavenger's daughter, and other instruments of torture used to spread the Religion of Humanity : yet we must not judge all Christians by the evil deeds of a few men, nor call Christianity a fungus because villains have traded in its doctrines.

In establishing Mormonism, as in founding many other religions, some people became members because it afforded an opportunity to gratify ambition, to attain notoriety, to hold the reins of power, and to amass a vast fortune through the credulity of ignorant believers. Some, attracted by what to them was license, simulated belief, and under the garb of hypocrisy revelled in the satisfaction of their grossest passions. Others were in-telligent but emotional, and when once convinced—partly perhaps by defective reasoning, and partly by sensation—that they found truth in this particular phase of religious life, they never wavered, and still cling to their belief, blinded by the effects of early training or fanatical emotion.

SWAYED BY SOPHISTRY.

But the rank and file of the saints belong to none of these classes. They are from the great body of illiterate persons, who, being awed at realising that they are in a world of mystery, if born in any land under the sun would succumb to the strongest local religious influence. The ranks of all churches are recruited from their midst, and any smart and unscrupulous man can sway them by specious words, until they are ready to accept sophistry as the inspired word of God. People of this kind have for ages being maintaining by the sweat of their brows, indolent and hypocritical professional teachers of religion, and will continue to do so until we stray much farther from the Missing Link, or until Faith is lost in Sight of the Eternal.

"JUDGE NOT THAT YE BE NOT JUDGED."

If we set ourselves up as Judges of the morality of individuals whose environment differs widely from our own, we are guilty of the sin of uncharitableness, and we arrogate to ourselves what we do not possess, viz., a perfect knowledge of the operations of those wonderful faculties with which man has been endowed. The power of hereditary tendencies; the peculiarities of temperament; the effects of association with good and evil, which is inseparable from active participation in the struggle for existence; the influence of inexplicable, and perhaps ungovernable impulses, and the force of temptation—all these go to make up the complexity of our natures and actions; and until we stand at the Eternal Bar of Justice we shall never know the exact extent of the moral accountability of any man, be he Mormon or Mahommedan, Murderer or Monarch.

If you decide that all men have absolute free-will, abide by your own decision, and remember that if there is an infallible standard of morality preached to you, you will be morally responsible for every violation of its code. If then your life is not perfect in action as well as in intention, remember that, not being without sin, you must not cast the first stone at another frail mortal.

If, on the contrary, you admit that those who fain would do right ' are conscious most of wrong within,' and that will power and intellectual comprehension are both limited by external and hereditary influences, you must then hold out the warm hand of fellowship to those whose lives apparently contain more blots than those of persons who have been swayed by more enlightening forces.

Meet the Mormon as a member of the great family of humanity ; respect the good in him ; sympathise with natural limitations of understanding, and try to convince him that there is a greater good than that which he has heretofore perceived. Above all do not let the following lines by Ella Wheeler Wilcox be true in your case :—

TWO WOMEN.

I know two women ; and one is chaste
And cold as the snow on a winter waste ;
Stainless ever, in act and thought
(As a man born dumb in speech errs not).
But she has malice toward her kind—
A cruel tongue and a jealous mind.
She judges the world by her narrow creed,
And never performs a kindly deed ;
A brewer of quarrels, a breeder of hate,
Yet she holds the key to Society's gate.

The other woman with a heart of flame
Went mad for a love that marred her name ;
But out of the grave of her murdered faith
She rose like a soul that has passed thro' death.
Her aim is noble, her pity so broad
It covers the world like the mercy of God.
A healer of discord, a soother of woes,
Peace follows her footsteps wherever she goes
The worthier life of the two, no doubt ;
And yet Society locks her out.

CHAPTER XIX.

———

"Society is arriving at the consciousness that for an ordinary woman to expect the monopoly of a man of genius is a crime of vanity and of egotism so enormous that it cannot be accepted in its pretensions or imposed upon him in its tyranny."

—OUIDA.

"As the word of God has declared marriage to be honourable in all, so we must infer that His laws have made provision for the honourable marriage of all, and that every person of each sex is equally entitled to its rights and benefits. If love be refining and ennobling, if it be the spontaneous instinctive birthright of all, and if our Creater has restricted its indulgence to the marriage relation, then marriage must be the right of all, or else God is not a benevolent being. The fault is not in nature, nor in the laws of God; but it is in the tyrannical laws and fashions of the artificial system of social life which now obtains among us."

THE HISTORY AND PHILOSOPHY OF MARRIAGE.

———

IS POLYGAMY IMMORAL?

IS polygamy immoral, or must we only judge it on the grounds of expediency?

We know that systems of morals are built up on what ought to be; so that an action which will in all probability be productive of greater harm than good, is classed as immoral. If an act, however, is not necessarily productive of evil, but *may be* because of the attitude of a man's 'little world' towards it, it may be inexpedient, but cannot reasonably be considered immoral. A girl may wear a low-necked ball dress in a ball-room with the greatest propriety; yet if she appeared in this attire on the street Society would be so shocked that it might blast her reputation. Many little things will occur to the reader which hinge upon expediency alone. If the individual were alone on a desert island no harm would result; yet every day we resign a certain amount of liberty of action, not because we should do wrong, but rather because our deeds might have the appearance of evil to persons who, being differently constituted, could not conscientiously do the same thing. If we persistently entirely disregard conventionality, we may not feel condemned, and yet our example may, like a stone flung in water, set in motion ripples whose circles will expand until they enter many a life with injurious results. A great reform, if introduced suddenly and inopportunely, would perhaps carry with it an incalculable amount of evil, counter-balancing the general good tendency of the scheme.

POLYGAMY RESPECTABLE.

In the times of Abraham, Solomon and David, when polygamy and concubinage were recognised institutions, it would have been absurd to stigmatise them as immoral. Conscientious and religious people, I contend, might practise plural marriage voluntarily, and their sincerity and self-sacrificing spirit *might* eliminate grossness from it, so that *under these conditions* it might be a distinct good. But when we come to contrast plural marriage with monogamy, bearing in mind the imperfections of human nature, we may find that the latter is vastly superior to the former, because, all things considered, the one man one wife system produces greater good, with less demand upon the restraint of those who adopt it.

MORMON TEMPLE AND TABERNACLE.

I regard polygamy as inexpedient rather than immoral, because the common-sense of mankind has abandoned it, and because we could not ordinarily furnish the conditions under which it might be looked upon as natural, workable and beneficial.

We are told that in Japan free love (or a mixture of promiscuous intercourse and polyandry) is an honoured institution, and that—

" After 2,000 years of free love . . . . . we find crime rare, the prisons almost empty, domestic tragedies nearly unknown, adultery uncommon ; very few foundlings thrown upon public charity, all children being at the father's charge . . . . . In no country in the world are political and social order more complete ; in none it seems is there more life-long conjugal felicity." •

Here it will be seen is an institution less rigid than polygamy, alleged to produce beneficial results because of the attitude of the Japanese nation towards it. We have no greater right to condemn their system as being immoral, than they have to seek to compel us to adopt free love in England. In all probability Mrs. Zina Young was right when she said that their object in practising polygamy was not to pander to base passions, but to bring into the world many righteous children. There is no allegation, either, that in a Mormon community the horrors of prostitution abound, as they do in other communities, because Mormonism has rigid laws by which it regulates the lives of its believers.

Inequalities of intellectual grasp and varieties of temperament help to form various customs in particular localities and different ages. Polygamy served its purpose, and we discard it only because we find another kind of sexual relation is more in harmony with our complex society and modern conditions of life.

WHAT DOES THE BIBLE SAY?

Still there are many persons who would regard plural marriage as immoral if the Bible condemns it. Field's Revised Handbook of Theology says that the Bible contains an infallible standard of morality. If direct condemnation of it is found in the Scriptures, no doubt the majority of English people would argue that this establishes its immorality. This, however, is not the case.

After carefully referring to numerous passages in the Scriptures under the indexed heads of " Polygamy disapproved of," " Laws concerning Marriage," and " Its nature and design," I am bound to say that Mrs. Young was strictly accurate when she told me that nowhere in the Old or New Testaments is there a word positively condemning plural marriage as a sin. Under the Mosaic dispensation polygamy was extensively practised, and although adultery and other crimes in relation to the sexes were punishable with death, yet polygamy is treated as though it were a legitimate and moral institution. In the 21 chap. Deut. the law is laid down that *if a man have two wives,* one of whom he hates and the other he loves, and if the hated one's child is the first-born, he must not be deprived of his greater share of inherited property on account of that hatred. Solomon is not censured for having 700 wives and 300 concubines; but because they were women from idolatrous nations, who led him astray from the Jewish religion in his old age. And though Solomon lays down wise precepts, many of which are applicable to all ranks and conditions of men, all nationalities, and all times, he does not deal with the peculiar Oriental harem life as compared or contrasted with a monogamous system of marriage. The only bone of contention is the common use of the singular, instead of the plural number in the Scriptures; and such language as " And they twain shall be one flesh."

But generally speaking, biblical laws tend to show that it was optional for a man to live with one wife or a dozen, provided they were not other men's wives, or connected by ties of consanguinity, or were not idolators.

CHRIST SILENT ON THE SUBJECT.

In the New Testament it is somewhat remarkable that Christ is only said to have spoken once at any length concerning Marriage, and then mainly confined himself to condemning divorce for any cause except adultery. He uses the term "wife" and not " wives," but although Josephus says " for it is with us an ancient practice to have many wives at the same time," Christ does not say that this practice was either immoral or productive of unhappiness. Paul, in his epistles, " speaking by permission and not of commandment," while recommending celibacy in some instances, does not denounce polygamy.

Practically then we have no decisive scriptural grounds for considering plural marriage repugnant to God or man, if the contract is voluntary, and the woman only has one husband; while the latter does not prove unfaithful, or seek divorce except on the ground of the woman's adultery.

We have then, I contend, to try polygamy as expedient or inexpedient—not moral or immoral. Is it equal or superior to Monogamy? Would it be productive of greater happiness? Is it necessary in order to eradicate any existing evils?

THE HISTORY OF MARRIAGE.

A glance at the history of marriage will help us to answer these enquiries. Bagehot, in his " Physics and Politics," states that promiscuous intercourse was the first form of sexual relationship between primitive man and woman. Organised society was then unknown, and a mutual desire for pleasure was all that was necessary, and no marriage laws existed. Descent was traced through the mother alone. When population increased and the units were welded together—the association being for mutual protection and assistance—restraints had to be imposed on individuals in order that the public safety might be promoted. Free intercourse was superseded by polygamy, which was succeeded by monogamy as the intelligence of the community increased and a higher standard was set up. Sir J. William Dawson, however, in " Points of Contact between Revelation and Natural Science," furnishes a crushing answer to this theory, and affirms that deviations from monogamous relationship have been lapses from the original marriage state, and that consequently the ideal of modern advocates of free love and polygamy is not only an inferior one, but contrary to the intention of the Creator of the Universe.

In the chapter on " Primitive Social Institutions," he says :—

" Certain archæologists have recently been much occupied with attempts to trace the social condition of primitive man in the customs of the ruder and more barbaric tribes, and in turn to deduce these from a supposed bestial condition in which the family and the marriage tie did not exist. Now, it is well known that in countries so widely separated as North America, India, Australia, and New Guinea, we find certain peculiar and often complex laws of affinity and of marriage, which are probably of very ancient origin. These are such as the following :—The recognition of woman as the principal factor in the family; descent in the female line, and systems of consanguinity based on this ; exogamy, or prohibition to marry within the same tribe or family ; family tokens or emblems devised to regulate these arrangements, and in connection with all this, a system of tribal communion, in which the wives and mothers are a related communism, into which the husbands are introduced from without by the practice of exogamy.

" That this complicated system sprang from a primitive promiscuous intercourse is a pure assumption and contrary to scientific probability. The long period of helplessness and dependence of the human child renders it essential that the relation of husband and wife should have existed from the first; or to place the matter on the lowest level, that man should be a permanently pairing animal, and the analogy of some of the animals nearest to man, though the nearest of these are very remote from him in this respect, strengthens this conclusion. Again, so soon as men formed tribes and communities, which necessity would oblige them to do almost from the first, it would become necessary to guard the family relation, and this was done by enforcing the rights of the wife and mother to her husband and her child, and to care and protection in child-bearing and nursing. Lastly the law of exogamy could scarcely have been spontaneous, but must have been an expedient devised by sagacious leaders in order to prevent, on the one hand, too close inter-marriage ; and, on the other, entire isolation on the part of the tribes into which men were necessarily divided, and at the same time to avert undue variation and degradation. In the record of the social arrangements of primitive man as given in the Bible, we have intimations of these institutions, and confirmations of their existence in subsequent references, even after the patriarchal and tribal arrangements had been fully established."

Further on this writer says, " Not long ago, a late eminent archæologist was surprised when I pointed out to him that his discoveries of exogamy and descent in the female line had been anticipated in the law ' therefore shall a man leave his father and mother and shall cleave unto his wife.' Here it is the husband who leaves his family to go with his wife, and she, as the centre of the family and mother of the children, is the true husband, bond of the household . . . . . . ' In the village community the women rule ; in the tribe or clan there is a patriarchal chief."

If detailed reasons as to why polygamy should not be regarded as the highest form of sexual relationship are requisite, they can easily be adduced. Here are some which, I consider effectually prove the case for monogamy as against plural marriage :—

WHY POLYGAMY IS INEXPEDIENT.

First, because of our antagonistic ideas, which are the result of our modern training and expansion of thought. We do not live in a land where polygamy is an " honoured institution," and however we may have imbibed the antagonistic sentiment, it is repugnant to at least the female sex, and to a large proportion of men. Unless there are certain specific advantages to be derived from an enforced revulsion of feeling we should be foolish to abandon our present system, but rather seek to renovate it whenever necessary. We do not believe that God commands us through Joseph Smith to re-institute polygamy, or that the more children we have the greater will be our crown of glory in the other world. If we adopted polygamy at all it would be because we considered it innately superior to monogamy, which it is not.

Second, because a religious belief in its necessity seems indispensable, as the Mormons admit that human nature being selfish, only a strong sense of religious duty can enable a woman to overcome her aversion to only retaining a section of her husband's affections.

Third, because from an economic standpoint there is no necessity for such an increase in the population as would follow if polygamy were to become universal. In fact the present rate of increase in a country where monogamy is the rule is becoming a serious problem for social reformers; as selfish competition, leading to an inequality in the distribution of wealth, has produced wide-spread poverty. Even a deluge of " righteous " children after the Mormon type, would not be hailed as an unmixed blessing.

Fourth, because even if competition were abolished, and the production of wealth became even greater than it is at present, by co-operation, each individual's share of the annual profits would not suffice to maintain more than one wife and family. Under our present industrial system polygamy is only possible to the rich.

If plural marriage be admitted to be a desideratum it is absurd and unjust that the wealthy man should monopolise several women and the poor man have only one.

Fifth, because even if men could afford it, there would not be enough women to go round in large numbers. The proportion of male births to females throughout the world is said to be as twenty-one to twenty, but war and other causes turn the scales slightly the other way as people grow older. Consequently the principle could not be of universal application.

FAULT IN MEN, NOT THE SYSTEM.

Sixth, because the adoption of polygamy would not necessarily mean the abolition of prostitution. It is true that many women remain single now who might be happier married, and many would not lead immoral lives if they could marry a man ; but compulsory single life does not usually lead to prostitution on the part of women, nor is single life caused by the prevalence of prostitution. The reasons why many young men and women remain unmarried are varied, usually being economic or personal. Poverty frequently prevents marriage. Inability to find a suitable partner in life acts similarly. A selfish desire for gratification of the passions, without bearing any of the burdens of paternity, actuates as a barrier in other cases. Prostitution of women result more frequently from an inordinate craving for fine garments, indolence, defective moral training, (resulting in dissipation and drunkenness,) betrayal by a lover, and other causes; rather than from the necessity of earning a livelihood by bartering the body for gold.

The same cause which now makes a man unfaithful to his one wife would make him discontented with any number of wives, and he would ever be on the look out for fresh faces. Turkish harems would spring up all over the land among those who would accept the burden of maintaining a large number of wives. But the men who are now single because they are too poor, or because they cannot find even one suitable partner in life, would not be benefited by being privileged to have a dozen unsuitable ones if they could maintain them. So that there would still be an enormous number of single women who would have to earn their own living; and even if from this cause single women often led immoral lives, (which I deny) there would be little diminution in the number of prostitutes. I have shown what are some of the more frequent causes of prostitution, and these would not be removed were polygamy to be sanctioned by law and public opinion.

If, as is claimed by Mrs. Zina Young, the Mormon men and women are rigidly faithful to each other, and there is no immoral class maintained in Salt Lake City, this is because the Mormons are governed by a religious sentiment and belief, and a sense of duty. This has a tendency to change people's nature, but if religion were separated from polygamy, and human nature left as it is at the present time, those who are impure would be impure still.

Seventh, because polygamy requires a much greater amount of self-sacrifice on the part of women than men. Love seems naturally to beget jealousy, and where there is no jealousy there is a lack of desire to be together, arising from an absence of personal interest, which can be traced back to a lack of love. Under polygamy a woman is required to be content to know, not only that her husband is not with her, but that at a particular time he is caressing another woman. In return for this suppression of her feelings what does the man sacrifice? He has a larger amount of self-indulgence than before, in return for supporting a greater number of wives, which many men would gladly do provided they had the means. He would have a dozen homes instead of one, and Society would regard his actions as perfectly proper, although each wife would undoubtedly feel an instinctive bitterness at being deserted so frequently; and the chances are that the less attractive wives would be treated with growing indifference, while each new addition to the vineyard would temporarily possess almost a monopoly of the man's attentions.

Eighth, because if a man had numerous wives, and a family of forty or fifty children, like Brigham Young for instance, there would almost inevitably be an absence of paternal love and training. A man could hardly keep track of their names, much less study their individual characteristics in order to secure their esteem, and help to develop their varied tastes and talents. Our home training in England is defective enough, but what it would be if polygamy prevailed is a prospect scarcely pleasant to contemplate.　　　　O 2

MONOGAMY A SUPERIOR INSTITUTION.

Ninth, because under a monogamous system we can remove any evils or cure any defects, more successfully than under a polygamous system. We have all the advantages which arise in the latter state, if there are any, and many others in addition, notwithstanding that only recently it has been shown that in many cases English marriage is a failure; for the same deplorable results would follow, and more rapidly, if polygamy were the rule. If one man and one woman could not live together without being miserable, would there not be greater discord if the man had to please twelve women, and they had to divide his love between them?

Tenth, because a man should be governed by Duty as much as a woman. If he denies that variety (otherwise promiscuous intercourse) is desirable in her case, why should he not be required to exercise similar self-restraint? And is it not his duty to seek to make her happy? If parties are unhappily mated, we might sanction greater freedom of divorce rather than doom two individuals to life-long misery; but we could not approve of the introduction of a system which would only aggravate the evil. It is less burdensome for men and women to live in monogamy happily and chastely than in polygamy. What kind of men are they who usually violate our marriage laws? Are they the finest specimens of manhood, or do they not usually lack love, sympathy, honour, and manliness? A man who is impulsive and subject to wandering fancies for other women, will restrain himself if he has a sincere regard for his wife, and will also treat her with consideration even though he may not consider that less restricted sexual relations would be immoral. But if a man will play the hypocrite now and endanger his wife's health, he would give the freest reign to his fancies and passions, if he could do so with the sanction of Society and the permission of a self-sacrificing wife.

Eleventh, because if monogamy is not perfect, it is far more preferable than polygamy. Monogamy " furnishes the conditions under which the highest specimens of human nature are evolved ; it has given us ideally perfect unions of man and woman." We have the home, the family, with conjugal and parental love in a marriage state which is best adapted for perpetuating the race and ensuring the public weal. There is ample opportunity for unselfishness in our system, if it is claimed that Mormonism is good because it develops that quality.

SELF-GOVERNMENT THE CURE.

We must not expect to gather grapes of thorns or figs of thistles. We should not consider that our system is necessarily defective, or that another is preferable, merely because men do not try to govern their inclinations, or plead that desire alone must be recognised and satisfied. If free-will is not altogether a delusion, then men can (particularly if a religious sentiment is cultivated) keep their passions within the boundary of a monogamous marriage ; and if a remedy for an evil which is the result of selfish animal cravings is sought outside of the cultivation of a higher moral sense, it will be as futile as expecting to abolish poverty without placing a check on man's selfishness, and without equalising incomes.

We should be sympathetic to the impulsive, and seek to lift them when they have fallen, rather than encourage them to repeat the act by sanctioning it. The Mormons should not be condemned or persecuted if they are conscientious, and are not trying to force others into their mode of life. But the public must guard against being carried away by fanaticism, or even milder emotionalism and defective reasoning. Freedom of thought, speech, and action, should be granted to all, except when it is palpable that such a course would lead to vice or crime. We should aim at the highest and best line of life, and remember that as an integral part of Society it is our duty to abstain from many things not because they are rigidly *wrong*, but only inexpedient.

OUR ATTITUDE TO MORMONISM.

It may seem hard to the Mormons that they should be imprisoned for doing what they believe to be right; but still, viewing all sides of the case, I can but think that the United States Government is right and consistent in preventing the practise of polygamy, just as it prohibits bigamy or other illegal acts. It would be preferable if a punishment could be devised to distinguish criminals who do wrong with the full consciousness that it *is* wrong, from religious zealots who violate modern ideas of good conduct through a sincere belief that they are doing what is right in the sight of God. At present the only course open seems to be to discountenance plural marriage because of the probable effect it would have on the rising generation.

The latest advices from Utah (September 16th, 1890) state that " Judge Anderson, in sentencing a large number of Mormons for polygamy at the September term of the Second District Court, held at Beaver, in this State, remarked upon the fact that all the accused had refused to promise to obey the laws in future; yet the Mormons constantly caused it to be reported through the Press and in Congress that polygamy had been abandoned. The fact was, he said, that the Mormons proclaimed abroad that polygamy was not practised in Utah, while that every term a crowd of polygamous offenders were sentenced to terms of imprisonment, and refused to even promise to obey the laws in future. The pretensions of the Mormons, the judge concluded, were false and absurd."

This shows the difficulties with which the judicial authorities have to cope, and the obstinacy of the Mormons; but we must not forget, however, that harsh measures are not altogether satisfactory. Only in a certain degree can we counteract erratic ideas by legislative enactments. Unless we appeal to the intelligence, and convince individuals that the thing condemned is unworthy of acceptance and adoption, rigid laws will be only partially successful.

HACKING A SHADOW.

It will not do to imitate the example of the Methodists and Campbellites, who are said to have once mobbed Joseph Smith and treated him to a dose of tar and feathers. As Mr. Rowland says:—" History affords few more striking examples of the powerlessness of persecution to put down even mistaken faith, than that exhibited by Mormonism. It would be as easy to hack a shadow with a Damascus blade as to cut down a superstition by the use of physical force."

It is a great mistake to imagine that Mormonism is dying out. Persecution gave new life to Christianity; and any unnecessary restraint of the liberties of Mormons should be avoided. It is unwise to foster the idea that they are martyrs, and their judges brutal enemies. The great cure for ignorance is education; the remedy for a dwarfed system of morality, one that is superior. " If we would deal with the evils in systems we must do so by purifying the issues of moral thought, not by attempting to constrain it by legal impedimenta." The more light that is thrown on the defects in the system, and the loftier the motives advocated as guiding forces in life, the more beneficial will be the results.

THE LATEST MANIFESTO.

Will the President of the Mormon Church be true to his word? He has just issued a manifesto dated October 6th, 1890, to the effect that the Church teaches polygamy no longer. This act is said to be the outcome of a special revelation from God. He also declares his intention of submitting to the law of the United States prohibiting plural marriages. If he abide by this decision, and his flock obey the voice of the Shepherd, the most objectionable feature of Mormonism will have been renounced.

THE END.

PRINTED BY HOBLYN & TAYLER, THE CORNWALL PRINTING WORKS, REDRUTH.

www.ingramcontent.com/pod-product-compliance
Lightning Source LLC
Chambersburg PA
CBHW030827270326
41928CB00007B/938